# Lean Beach Cuisine

*A Collection of Healthy Coastal Recipes.*
*by Jewel Cammarano*

**FATHER & SON**
PUBLISHING, INC.
4909 N. Monroe Street
Tallahassee, Florida 32303
http://www.fatherson.com

# Dedication

I dedicate this book to my parents.

# ACKNOWLEDGMENTS

I WISH TO THANK JOHN, FOR HIS UNENDING LOVE AND SUPPORT

JOHN JR. AND REGINA, FOR THEIR AWESOME PRIDE IN ME

MARY-KAY FOR HER BEAUTIFUL COVER-ART

HUGH FOR HIS LITERARY CONTRIBUTION

CAROL, FOR HER FRIENDSHIP AND HELP IN EDITING THIS BOOK

AND ESPECIALLY LANCE, WITHOUT WHOM THIS BOOK
WOULD NOT BE PUBLISHED

# Table of Contents

# INTRODUCTION

I have always lived near a beach. I don't know what stroke of fate has dealt me such good fortune, but my days have always begun looking to the east, waiting for the sun to rise over a blue body of ocean. Such has been my orientation since my very first memories as a young child. I am a nutritionist and have worked since my very first career, in many and varied areas of foods and nutrition. Both field of food and the science of nutrition hold a fascination for me; a fascination as strong as the love I feel for the sea.

This union of love for food and the beach has been instrumental for me. In my first book *BEACH CUISINE,* I explored the Atlantic coast with a collection of recipes from places on that coastline that held special memories. Indeed, they evolved over many years and became a unique cuisine in their own right. They were the result of southern and regional influence, sometimes what was available and many times what came out of the sea. In *LEAN BEACH CUISINE* I have taken recipes one step further. A lot of waves have crashed over the sand for me since the concept of a cuisine for the beach first began in my mind. Many trips to the shore, more beach vacations to different coastal destinations, cooking 'beach cuisine', wonderful gourmet restaurants by the sea, more cooking 'beach cuisine'—and high cholesterol! My education and experience have taught me one thing well—most of us can control the factors that influence our optimal health by controlling what we eat. Given that good health is often taken for granted, it is one of the most precious gifts in life, but it can not be maintained without good eating habits and a healthy weight. These two factors alone, when controlled can reduce one's risk for many health problems and diseases. For me, this had to mean my beach cuisine had to be *lean.*

You have just opened a cookbook that is not like any other. Cuisine at the beach is a celebration for eating. It is summertime, cool breezes and refreshing drinks; it is barbecues and oyster roasts, with aromas of grilled food intermingling with the fresh ocean air; it is crisp veggies and aromatic herbs that have been kissed by a golden sun, fresh fish just caught from the sea. And above all—it is lean! For those who live along our coastal shores or travel to and vacation there, the recipes in this book may tantalize your memory banks with flavors and tastes from the beach; and like a breath of fresh ocean air, bring back to you associations you may have with these special places. If a trip to the shore is a rare event, then you may allow these recipes to capture you and take you on a culinary tour of our capacious coastlines. Coast to coast and shore to shore, you will be amazed that the bright fresh ingredients and full-flavored tastes which characterize these 196 recipes can be healthy and wholesome—and be so delicious too!

*LEAN BEACH CUISINE* is not a diet book. If there is one thing the world has enough of, it is diet plans and as we know, for most people diets don't work. This book is a tool to be used, by which you can cook and eat in a healthy way. It is a style of cooking that uses ingredients that are naturally wholesome and fresh, full-flavored and healthy. The cooking techniques are simple and unpretentious, but will produce gourmet meals. When I was choosing recipes for this book, I wanted them to be representative of regional areas along all of our coastlines from Maine to Florida, along the gulf coast and up the entire stretch of the Pacific. Writing recipes with a personal connection to their region made working on this book so exciting. I will never forget how many times I cooked stuffed calamari after I had tasted a similar preparation in a small restaurant on the Monterey peninsula in California. It got better every time, until I couldn't improve upon it anymore. I was thrilled to come up with a dipping sauce for Maine lobster that wasn't only pure butter, but a blend of flavors to die for. I was amazed to find such ethnic diversity in our American coastal cuisine. International, traditional southern, Cajun, Mexican, Oriental and Italian influences—they are all here, lightened up and making this collection of coastal recipes so rich and so varied. A traveloque of seashore delights, *LEAN BEACH CUISINE* is a volume to be treasured by the health conscious cook who loves sunrises and sunsets, no matter what coast they are on.

## NUTRITION AND YOUR HEALTH

Healthy eating is your best personal investment. Many studies prove that people in countries who consume the healthiest diets consisting of whole grains, fruits, vegetables and low-fat protein enjoy a longer life expectancy and a reduced risk for heart disease, stroke, diabetes, cancer and other diseases. In the United States, obesity has increased in recent years at an alarming rate. In our land of plenty where the burger is king and dairy is queen, our super-fast pace of life has taken us out of our kitchens and into restaurants and fast food joints for many of our meals. We super-size our portions, indulge in too much saturated fat and are wearing the results around our waistlines, while our risk factors for disease are adding up.

For many battling with a weight problem, diets don't work. Every diet has it's own form of built-in deprivation and some enslave it's victims into tedious counting of calories and fat grams. Some diets are nothing but gimmicks and are based on no proven scientific studies. Worse yet, some diets are downright unhealthy to live on! Dieting, however, seems to be America's number one preoccupation in life. It is a million dollar industry that ensnares countless victims every day in order to separate them from their money. If you doubt this is true, you need only to go into the nearest bookstore and count the volumes of diet books found on the shelves. Sadly, many people give up an already unhealthy diet, only to replace it with some unreal mania for eating unnaturally for the sake of a temporary weight loss, that in most instances is only regained. Without thinking, the willingness to rob the body of a balanced diet that supplies all of the nutrients necessary for metabolic processes takes priority in the hopes that fat will magically melt away, even at the cost of our nutritional well-being. Taking this into consideration, it is easy to conclude that dieting is detrimental to the state of our general health.

I don't believe in diets. I am not referring to individuals for whom certain health problems and medical conditions may dictate food restrictions as necessary and a matter of life or death, but to the rest of us—those of us who enjoy the grace of good health and who at times, may abuse it. For these are the majority of us and we all know better. For the last twenty years in the United States, science has made tremendous progress in the field of nutrition and this is just the beginning. We hear every day on the media the basic lesson of eating an unhealthy diet. The studies are numerous and all in agreement that the amount of fat and calories in our typical American diet plays a major role in raising blood cholesterol leading to obesity, heart disease and stroke. We are a "fat conscious society" more today than ever, yet we continue to gain weight.

For these multitudes, it is obvious that we have removed ourselves from some very basic premises and have simply over complicated the formula to good nutrition. When did it become so difficult? Well, it doesn't have to be. I believe the word 'diet' should be defined to 'a lifetime plan for healthy eating'. We have known all along, somewhere in our memory banks that a healthy diet is very logical and purely a matter of arithmetic. It all boils down to common sense—eat a variety of foods that appear in all food groups and do so in moderation. A lifetime plan for healthy eating is instrumental in order to maintain a healthy body weight. Body weight is maintained when you eat the same number of calories that you burn in a given day. When you take in more calories than the body needs, you gain weight and conversely, when you eat less, you lose—a matter of simple arithmetic. Easy, isn't it?

O.K., so it's not! The simple principles above for a healthy lifetime eating plan most certainly have influencing factors to consider. It matters whether we are male or female, what age we are, what our activity level is and whether the fat we eat in our diet is saturated, unsaturated or poly-unsaturated and how much of it we consume. The optimal formula for a healthy eating plan for each individual certainly needs some management and fortunately, we have some help.

# DIETARY GUIDELINES AND THE
# FOOD GUIDE PYRAMID

The United States Department of Agriculture has set up dietary guidelines to meet the needs of all healthy individuals. As researchers learn more about the relationship between food and health, they can help people make better food selections to maintain and improve well being. The US Recommended Dietary Allowances (RDAs) were developed by the Food and Nutrition Board of the National Academy of Sciences National Research Council. The RDAs give recommendations for adequate levels of nutrients needed by the average person based on age and sex. The USDA suggests that a person's daily calorie intake should not exceed 30% of calories consumed in fat. Based on a 2,000 calorie diet these guidelines would fall into the following percentages:

| | |
|---|---|
| calories | 2,000 |
| protein | 15% |
| fat | 30% or less |
| carbohydrate | 50% |
| cholesterol | 300 mg. |
| sodium | 2400 mg. |

The Food Guide Pyramid is a pictorial representation of the guidelines above. Using the Food Guide Pyramid will help you select foods with variety and moderation that will enable you to maintain and even improve your health. The Pyramid is made up of six food groups, with the placement of each group on the pyramid corresponding to the daily recommended number of servings for that group. The base of the pyramid is made up of the largest food group: breads, cereal, rice and pasta and calls for 6-11 servings. The next two groups on the pyramid are vegetables (3-5 servings) and fruits (2-4 servings). Higher up on the pyramid are the protein groups calling for 2-3 servings daily. They are the milk, yogurt and cheese group and the meat, poultry, fish, beans, eggs and nut group. The group that appears on the tip of the pyramid is comprised of fats, oils and sweets, which are recommended to be consumed sparingly.

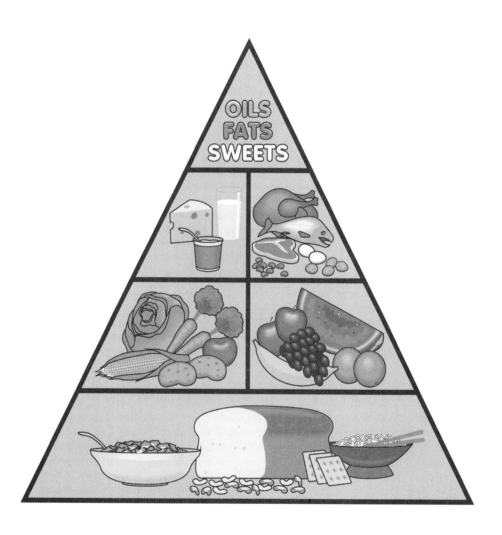

OILS
FATS
SWEETS

# A FINAL WORD

Healthy eating can be accomplished by using the *Food Pyramid Guide*. It is one of the tools when used with this book that will help make it easy for you. By choosing a varied and moderate eating plan with the majority of calories coming from fruits, vegetables, whole grains and low-fat protein, your personal diet will be a pattern to nutritious eating that will fit into any healthy lifestyle. The American Heart Association and the American Dietetic Association both recommend that you get at least half or fifty per-cent of your calories from carbohydrates (the lower group on the pyramid), thirty per-cent from fruits and vegetables and twenty per-cent of total calories from low-fat protein. They also recommend that fat consumption should not exceed thirty per-cent in the daily total food intake. You may choose to take these percentages into consideration and adjust them to fit your own health needs.

*Lean Beach Cuisine* will enable you to make healthy eating a delicious habit. Recipes in this book have been analyzed for their nutritional content using ESHA Research's Professional Nutritional Analysis Software. The data is given for one serving and the resulting information appears at the end of each recipe. Using these analyses you will see how all of the recipes fit within the guidelines of a healthy diet and how using them will help you to follow your own. You might note that we have used many low-fat and fat-free ingredients, but when you taste the results, you will see that we have not compromised the flavor. Each dish may certainly be made using the full-fat version of these ingredients; the choice is yours, but don't forget to add back the additional fat and calories into the total nutritional count. Hopefully, since recipes are guidelines for putting ingredients together, you may be inspired by this collection to create your own tastes. It doesn't take a genius to come up with simple substitutions for some of the items on these pages in order to invent a new and different flavor. You may even come up with ways to further improve the nutritional make-up of many favorites of your own. There is no mystery to healthy eating. Armed with your non-stick pan, vegetable cooking-spray, the nutritional tools above, the recipes in this book and your innovation, you will see that a healthy and delicious lifetime eating plan for you can be as easy and as much fun as a day at the beach! *Bon Appetit.*

# Appetizers & Beverages

# Appetizers & Beverages

## ALABAMA CHICKEN & CHEDDAR QUESADILLAS

| | |
|---|---|
| 8 | flour tortillas |
| 1 | (4-ounce) can chopped mild chiles |
| 2 | cups barbequed chicken, shredded |
| ½ | cup shredded low-fat Cheddar cheese |
| ½ | cup bottled taco sauce |
| 1 | cup salsa |
| ¼ | cup fat-free sour cream |
| | Cilantro for garnish |

Heat oven to 450°. Place one tortilla onto a large baking sheet. Spread with 1 tablespoon chopped chiles. Top with one quarter of chicken, cheese and taco sauce. Place another tortilla on top. Repeat with remaining tortillas, chiles, chicken, cheese and sauce, for a total of 4 separate quesadillas. Bake for 8 minutes, or until crispy and cheese has melted. Remove from oven, let stand for 5 minutes. Cut each quesadilla into quarters, garnish with cilantro, salsa and sour cream. Yield: 16 appetizers.

### Nutrition Facts

Per serving: Calories 256 (22% calories from fat) Fat 6 g (saturated fat 1.5 g) Protein 17 g Carbohydrates 32.5 g Fiber 1.25 g Cholesterol 33 mg Sodium 634 mg.

*Reduced-fat cheeses offer a 30-40% fat and calorie break from full-fatted versions. Find the brand you like by trying different ones. The health benefits will be worth it.*

# BRUSCHETTA WITH ROASTED PEPPERS

| | |
|---|---|
| 4 | roasted red bell peppers, peeled and seeded |
| 8 | ½-inch-thick slices of French or Italian bread |
| 2 | tablespoons finely chopped fresh basil |
| 1 | tablespoon balsamic vinegar |
| 1 | clove garlic, peeled and diced |
| | Salt and pepper to taste |
| 2 | ounces mozzarella, cut into thin strips |
| 2 | teaspoons olive oil |

Follow the recipe in this book for roasting peppers. Slice peppers into strips. Toast bread under broiler unit, until it browns. Turn bread and brown on other side.

In a medium bowl, combine peppers, basil, vinegar, garlic, salt and pepper to taste and toss gently. Arrange bread in a single layer on a roasting pan. Top with roasted peppers and lay mozzarella strips over the peppers. Drizzle with olive oil. Place bruschetta in a pre-heated broiler, about 6 inches from the heat source and broil until cheese melts and starts to brown. Serve immediately. Yield: 8 servings.

## Nutrition Facts

Per serving: Calories 103 (27% calories from fat) Fat 3 g (saturated fat 1 g) Protein 4 g Carbohydrates 15 g Fiber 2 g Cholesterol 4 mg Sodium 156 mg.

*To maintain healthy eating habits, don't fall for the "fat-free" trap. Cutting fat does not mean you can eat more. Doing so only increases your calorie intake and will still turn to fat.*

# CAPE SHOALWATER SMOKED SALMON

| | |
|---|---|
| 3½ | ounces smoked salmon, finely chopped |
| 2 | tablespoons light sour cream |
| 2 | teaspoons minced red onion |
| 1 | teaspoon drained capers |
| ½ | teaspoon prepared horseradish |
| ⅛ | teaspoon black pepper |
| ½ | ounce smoked salmon, thinly sliced |
| 24 | water crackers (or other) |
| | Extra capers for garnish |

In a medium mixing bowl, combine 3 ½ ounces salmon, sour cream, onion, capers and horseradish. Add pepper to season and set aside.

Cut ½ ounce thinly sliced smoked salmon into 24 square pieces. Place a dollop of salmon mixture onto each of 24 crackers and top with thin salmon slices. Garnish with extra capers and serve chilled. Yield: 24 appetizer crackers.

## Nutrition Facts

Per serving: Calories 38 (22% calories from fat) Fat 1 g (saturated fat .13 g) Protein 2 g Carbohydrates 6 g Fiber 0 mg Cholesterol 1.5 mg Sodium 142 mg.

*Fat-free crackers are great nibblers and a good way to satisfy the "crunch" cravings. Five crackers will only set you back about 50 calories.*

# CHESAPEAKE BLUE CRAB DIP

| | |
|---|---|
| 1 | (8-ounce) package fat-free cream cheese, softened |
| ¼ | cup evaporated skimmed milk |
| 2 | teaspoons lemon juice |
| 1½ | teaspoons Worcestershire sauce |
| ½ | pound blue crab meat, cooked |
| | Salt and pepper to taste |

Stir cream cheese until smooth. Gradually add milk, then stir in lemon juice and Worcestershire sauce. Carefully toss crab meat into mixture so as not to break up lumps. Season with salt and pepper; chill. Yield: 1 ½ cups or 6 servings.

## Nutrition Facts

Per serving: Calories 85 (13% calories from fat) Fat 1 g (saturated fat .4 g) Protein 14 g Carbohydrates 4 g Fiber 0 g Cholesterol 41 mg Sodium 339 mg.

# DESTIN DILLY VEGETABLE DIP

| | |
|---|---|
| 1 | cup fat-free sour cream |
| 1 | (8-ounce) package reduced-fat cream cheese, softened |
| 1 | tablespoon chopped chives |
| 1 | tablespoon chopped parsley |
| 1 | teaspoon dried onion flakes |
| 1 | teaspoon dried dill |
| ½ | teaspoon Worcestershire sauce |
| | Dash Tabasco sauce |
| | Salt to taste |

Blend sour cream and cream cheese together in a medium bowl. Add herbs and spices, Worcestershire and Tabasco. Blend well and refrigerate until ready to serve. This dip goes well with crackers, chips or fresh-cut vegetables. Yield: 2 cups (10-12 servings).

## Nutrition Facts

Per serving: Calories 68 (45% calories from fat) Fat 3.5 g (saturated fat 2 g) Protein 3.5 g Carbohydrates 5.5 g Fiber 0 g Cholesterol 12 mg Sodium 76 mg.

# FLORIDA STONE CRAB WITH MUSTARD DIPPING SAUCE

12     large stone crab claws, cooked (18 if they are small)
1      tablespoon prepared mustard
½     cup light mayonnaise
1      teaspoon Worcestershire sauce
1      tablespoon fat-free half & half
      Lettuce for garnish

Stone crab claws are cooked upon harvesting and may be purchased fresh or frozen. Store cooked claws in the refrigerator at 32-38 degrees F., or pack in ice no longer than two to three days. Frozen claws will thaw in the refrigerator in 12-18 hours. Do not thaw under running water, as quality will be lost. Keep stone crab claws refrigerated until ready to serve.

To prepare mustard dipping sauce, combine mustard, mayonnaise and Worcestershire sauce in a small bowl and whisk until smooth. Slowly add the half & half, continuing to whisk until the sauce reaches desired consistency. This sauce can be refrigerated until ready to use.

Prepare a serving dish by lining it with fresh crisp lettuce leaves. Arrange crab claws on top of lettuce around the outside edge of plate. Place dipping sauce in center of claws and serve immediately. Yield: 6 appetizer portions.

## Nutrition Facts

Per serving: Calories 195 (24% calories from fat) Fat 5 g (saturated fat 1 g) Protein 32 g Carbohydrates 3.5 g Fiber .5 g Cholesterol 77 mg Sodium 1580 mg.

*Mustard is low in fat and comes in many flavorful varieties. Add a little of your favorite one to sauces and dressings to add flavor and cut fat.*

# HOMEMADE BAGEL CHIPS

2   (4 ½-inch) whole-wheat bagels
    Herb seasoning
    Vegetable cooking spray

Use day-old bagels, if available. If not, a light oven-toasting will bring them to this stage. Using a sharp knife or a food processor, slice bagels vertically into thin rounds. Spread slices out in a single layer on a baking sheet. Sprinkle herb seasoning (or other desired seasoning blend) to cover in a light coating. Spray the seasoned rounds with vegetable cooking spray. Bake in a pre-heated 400° oven for 10 to 12 minutes, turning once, until they are golden on both sides. Use for dipping into your favorite dips and spreads. Yield: 6 servings.

## Nutrition Facts

Per serving: Calories 97 (4% calories from fat) Fat .5 g (saturated fat 0) Protein 4 g Carbohydrates 21 g Fiber 3.5 g Cholesterol 0 mg Sodium 197 mg.

*Tame a mighty bagel down to size. Instead of slicing in half, slice in thirds. Since most bagels are equal to 4 slices of bread, you will be doing yourself a favor. The thinner bagel slices will also fit into the toaster too.*

# GUACAMOLE FROM GALVESTON

| | |
|---|---|
| 1 | medium-size ripe avocado |
| ¾ | cup frozen green peas, thawed |
| 1 | tablespoon fresh lime juice |
| 2 | tablespoons chopped cilantro |
| ¼ | cup non-fat plain yogurt |
| 2 | tablespoons fat-free mayonnaise |
| ½ | cup chopped red onion |
| 1 | ripe tomato, seeded and diced |
| 1 | clove garlic, minced |
| ½ | teaspoon chili powder |
| | Desired amount of Tabasco sauce |
| | Salt to taste |

Peel the avocado and remove the seed. In a blender container, add the sliced avocado, peas, lime juice, cilantro, yogurt and mayonnaise. Puree until smooth. Put pureed mixture into a bowl and add onion, tomato, garlic and chili powder. Gently blend with a rubber spatula, until blended. Sprinkle with desired amount of Tabasco and season with salt to taste. Chill and serve with oven-baked tortilla chips for a really low-fat treat. Yield: 8 servings.

## Nutrition Facts

Per serving: Calories 68 (50% calories from fat) Fat 4 g (saturated fat .5 g) Protein 2 g Carbohydrates 7 g Fiber 2.5 g Cholesterol .5 mg Sodium 56 mg.

*Fat-free bean dips are so creamy, they don't taste fat-free. Delicious with raw vegetables or baked pita chips, they offer the bonus of added fiber and B vitamins with only 15 calories per tablespoon.*

# MARINATED SHRIMP FOR STARTERS

| | |
|---|---|
| 2 | pounds shrimp, steamed and peeled |
| ½ | purple onion, sliced into rings |
| 2 | tablespoons non-pariel capers |
| ¼ | cup canola oil |
| ½ | cup vinegar |
| 2 | teaspoons Worcestershire sauce |
| ½ | tablespoon Tabasco sauce |
| 1 | teaspoon sugar |
| 1 | teaspoon salt |
| ⅛ | teaspoon pepper |
| | Fresh parsley, chopped |

Place shrimp, onion rings and capers into a large shallow bowl. Combine canola oil, vinegar, Worcestershire, Tabasco, sugar, salt and pepper in a measuring cup. Mix and pour over shrimp. Refrigerate for 24 hours, stirring occasionally.

Remove to a serving dish with a slotted spoon. Cover the shrimp with onion rings and capers. Garnish with parsley and serve. Yield: 10 servings.

## Nutrition Facts

Per serving: Calories 155 (42% calories from fat) Fat 7 g (saturated fat .7 g) Protein 19 g Carbohydrates 3.5 g Fiber .33 g Cholesterol 138 mg Sodium 434 mg.

# NEW ORLEANS MUFFALETTA SPREAD

| | |
|---|---|
| 24 | stuffed green olives, chopped |
| 12 | extra-large pitted black olives, chopped |
| 2 | tablespoons roasted red peppers, chopped |
| 2 | tablespoons green bell peppers, chopped |
| 1 | tablespoon capers, drained and chopped |
| 2 | garlic cloves, minced |
| ¼ | cup chopped red onions |
| 1 | celery stalk, chopped finely |
| ¼ | cup fresh parsley, chopped |
| 1 | teaspoon dried oregano |
| ¼ | teaspoon black pepper |
| 2 | tablespoons balsamic vinegar |
| 2 | tablespoons olive oil |

Mix all ingredients together and let marinate in the refrigerator overnight. Use spread on your favorite cracker as an appetizer. Yield: 24 servings.

Note: Muffaletta spread is famous in the New Orleans French Quarter served on crusty bread loaves layered with salami, ham and provolone cheese.

## Nutrition Facts

Per serving: Calories 23 (76% calories from fat) Fat 2 g (saturated fat .2 g) Protein .2 g Carbohydrates 1.2 g Fiber .2 g Cholesterol 0 Sodium 134 mg.

*Spa nutritionists suggest splitting meal portions and saving part for snacking. Snacks don't have to be entirely different foods. This is one way to learn to love left-overs.*

# OCEAN CITY STEAMED CLAMS
# WITH SHERRY BROTH

| | |
|---|---|
| 36 | large raw clams |
| 3 | cups fat-free chicken broth |
| 2 | tablespoons butter |
| ½ | cup dry sherry wine |

    Scrub clams well under cold, running water to remove sand.  Place cleaned clams in a steamer pot with about 1 cup of water in the bottom.  Steam clams until they open, about 5 to 8 minutes.  Discard any that do not open.

    While clams are steaming, heat chicken broth in a small saucepan.  Bring to a boil and add butter and sherry.  Heat through and serve with clams as a dipping broth.  Yield: 6 servings.

## Nutrition Facts

Per serving:  Calories 151 (31% calories from fat)  Fat 5 g (saturated fat 2.5 g)
Protein 18.5 g  Carbohydrates 3.5 g  Fiber 0  Cholesterol 51 mg  Sodium 154 mg.

# OCEANSIDE OYSTERS CASINO

| | |
|---|---|
| 1 | pound fresh or frozen oysters |
| 3 | slices bacon, chopped |
| 4 | tablespoons chopped onion |
| 2 | tablespoons chopped green pepper |
| 2 | tablespoons chopped celery |
| 1 | teaspoon lemon juice |
| ½ | teaspoon Worcestershire sauce |
| ½ | teaspoon salt |
| ⅛ | teaspoon pepper |
| ⅛ | teaspoon hot pepper sauce |

Thaw oysters if frozen. Drain oysters. Remove any remaining shell particles. Place oysters in a 9x9x2-inch baking dish that has been sprayed with nonstick cooking spray.

Heat a medium-size saute pan over medium-high heat and cook bacon until crisp. Add onion, green pepper and celery. Cook vegetables until tender. Add lemon juice, Worcestershire sauce, salt, pepper and hot pepper sauce; mix well. Spread bacon mixture over oysters. Bake in a pre-heated 350° oven, about 10 minutes, or until edges of oysters begin to curl. Serves 6.

## Nutrition Facts

Per serving: Calories 120 (64% calories from fat) Fat 8.5 g (saturated fat 3 g) Protein 6.5 g Carbohydrates 4.3 g Fiber .25 g Cholesterol 48 mg Sodium 446 mg.

*Mix equal parts of unsweetened natural fruit juices with club soda or seltzer for a healthy and nutritious beverage.*

# OYSTERS ON THE HALF SHELL

6-8   oysters per person
Crushed ice
Favorite cocktail sauce
Lettuce leaves for garnish
Lemon or lime wedges

Scrub oyster shells thoroughly, with a firm brush under cold, running water. Shuck oysters, leaving oysters on one shell, and removing any bits of shell around the shucked oyster. Arrange the oysters on a bed of crushed ice, placing lettuce around the edges, if desired. Place a smaller bowl of cocktail sauce in center of serving dish, and place enough lemon or lime wedges around for each person.

## Nutrition Facts

Per serving: Calories 216 (22% calories from fat) Fat 5 g (saturated fat 1 g) Protein 20 g Carbohydrates 21 g Fiber .5 g Cholesterol 104 mg Sodium 820 mg.

# SARASOTA SHRIMP DIP

6    ounces small to medium shrimp, peeled and cooked
1    (8-ounce) package low-fat cream cheese, softened
2    tablespoons light mayonnaise
2    tablespoons chili sauce
1    tablespoon lemon juice
¼    teaspoon curry powder
      Fresh chopped parsley

Chop shrimp finely, then mash with a fork. In a medium bowl, toss the shrimp with the remaining ingredients, blending thoroughly. Refrigerate at least 2 hours before serving for flavors to blend. Just before serving, garnish with chopped parsley. Serve with crackers or chips. Yield: 2 cups (10 servings).

## Nutrition Facts

Per serving: Calories 82 (54% calories from fat)  Fat 5 g (saturated fat 2.5 g)
Protein 6 g  Carbohydrates 3.3 g  Fiber 0  Cholesterol 39 mg  Sodium 154 mg.

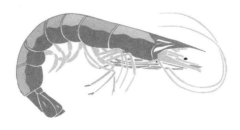

# SEAFARER'S CRAB FLAKE COCKTAIL

| | |
|---|---|
| 1 | pint fresh crabmeat, cooked |
| 1 | grapefruit |
| 3 | tablespoons orange juice |
| 4 | tablespoons catsup |
| ½ | teaspoon Worcestershire sauce |
| | Lettuce leaves |

Place freshly cooked crabmeat into a mixing bowl. Peel and cut grapefruit sections into small pieces and add to the crab. Blend orange juice, catsup and Worcestershire sauce, pour over crab mixture and toss to blend.

Line 4 well-chilled cocktail glasses or sherbet cups with lettuce leaves. Fill each with a generous portion of crab mixture. Serve with saltines or melba toast. Serves 4.

## Nutrition Facts

Per serving: Calories 101 (10% calories from fat) Fat 1.2 g (saturated fat 0) Protein 13 g Carbohydrates 10.5 g Fiber 1 g Cholesterol 59 mg Sodium 353 mg.

# SEA ISLE FRESH PEACH SALSA

| | |
|---|---|
| 3 | very ripe fresh peaches, skinned and chopped |
| 1 | large ripe garden tomato, peeled and chopped |
| ⅓ | cup diced red onion |
| 1 | small hot chile or jalapeno pepper, diced |
| ⅓ | cup peach preserves |
| 1 | tablespoon fresh lime juice |
| 1 | tablespoon sugar |
| ½ | teaspoon salt |
| ⅛ | teaspoon ground cumin |
| 1 | tablespoon chopped parsley |
| 1 | teaspoons minced cilantro (optional) |

Place chopped peaches and tomatoes into a medium mixing bowl. Add red onion and diced hot pepper, toss gently and set aside.

In a separate mixing bowl, stir preserves, lime juice, sugar, salt and cumin together. Add peach and tomato mixture and blend ingredients with a rubber spatula. Sprinkle with parsley and cilantro, if desired. Serve with your favorite chips. Yield: approxiamatley 1 pint (about 12 servings).

NOTE: To increase the heat for a spicier version, add cayenne pepper or hot sauce to taste.

## Nutrition Facts

Per serving: Calories 42 (2% calories from fat) Fat .1 g (saturated fat 0) Protein .4 g Carbohydrates 11 g Fiber .7 g Cholesterol 0 Sodium 103 mg.

*Salsas are a perky addition in flavor for grilled or broiled meat, fish or poultry. If you don't make your own, check labels for sodium content.*

# ST. AUGUSTINE'S CITRUS CEVICHE

| | |
|---|---|
| 1 | pound freshly caught red snapper fillets |
| ½ | cup fresh lemon juice |
| ¼ | cup fresh lime juice |
| ¼ | cup fresh orange juice |
| 1 | teaspoon grated fresh ginger |
| 1 | tablespoon olive oil |
| ¼ | cup chopped cilantro |
| 1 | small onion, thinly sliced |
| 1 | avocado, peeled, pitted and cut into chunks |

Chop the red snapper fillets into small chunks.  In a glass bowl combine the lemon juice, lime juice, orange juice, ginger and olive oil.  Add the fish and toss to coat.  Cover and marinate in the refrigerator for about 2 hours. The flesh of the fish should be white and opaque.

Add the cilantro, onion and avocado.  Season to taste with salt and pepper, toss and serve.  Yield: 8 appetizer servings.

NOTE:  Try this recipe with different kinds of fish.

## Nutrition Facts

Per serving:  Calories 122 (46% calories from fat)  Fat 6.5 g (saturated fat 1 g) Protein 11.5 g  Carbohydrates 5.5 g  Fiber 1.5 g  Cholesterol 20 mg  Sodium 38 mg.

# STUFFED CLAMS FROM BARNEGAT BAY

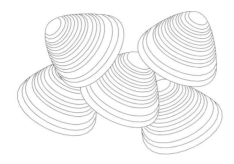

| | |
|---|---|
| 12 | large fresh clams, washed and scrubbed |
| ½ | cup frozen chopped spinach, defrosted and drained |
| 1 | cup fresh breadcrumbs |
| ¼ | cup fresh parsley, chopped |
| 2 | tablespoons Parmesan cheese |
| 2 | large garlic cloves, minced |
| | Salt and pepper to taste |
| 2 | tablespoons butter, melted |
| 1 | fresh lemon for its juice |

Place cleaned clams in a large bowl of ice water to allow them to open easily. When ready to bake, open each clam, reserving its natural juice. Place the half shells containing the clams on an oven-proof dish. Spoon a scant teaspoonful of spinach around each clam.

In a medium bowl, mix breadcrumbs, parsley, cheese, garlic, salt, pepper and melted butter together gently with a fork. Sprinkle each clam with breadcrumb mixture and drizzle fresh lemon juice on top. Bake in a 400^ oven for 10 minutes. Serve immediately. Yield: 6 appetizer portions.

## Nutrition Facts

Per serving: Calories 108 ( 42% calories from fat) Fat 5 g (saturated fat 2 g)
Protein 7 g Carbohydrates 9 g Fiber 1 g Cholesterol 16 mg Sodium 373 mg.

# ZESTY MESQUITE SMOKED SALSA

| | |
|---|---|
| 2 | cups mesquite chips |
| 1 | head garlic |
| 5 | plum tomatoes, cut in half lengthwise |
| 1 | medium onion, peeled and cut into rings |
| ½ | jalapeno pepper, seeded and cut lengthwise |
| 2 | large shallots, peeled and cut lengthwise |
| ¼ | cup chopped fresh cilantro |
| ¼ | cup fresh lime juice |
| ¼ | teaspoon salt |

Soak mesquite chips in water 30 minutes, then drain. Wrap chips in heavy-duty aluminum foil, and make several holes in foil. Light gas grill on one side; place foil-wrapped chips directly on hot coals. Coat grill rack on opposite side with cooking spray and place rack over cool lava racks. Let grill heat 10-15 minutes.

While the grill heats, peel outer skin from garlic; cut off and discard top one-third of garlic head. Place garlic (cut side up), tomato halves (cut side down), onion rings, shallots and jalapeno pepper in a grill basket. Place grill basket on rack on *opposite* side from hot coals; cover and cook 30 minutes. Turn vegetables; cover and cook 30 minutes more, or until vegetables are tender and lightly browned.

Remove vegetables from grill. Squeeze out pulp from each clove garlic. Position knife blade in food processor bowl; add garlic pulp and vegetables. Process until coarsely chopped, scraping sides of bowl once. Transfer vegetables to a small bowl; add cilantro, lime juice and salt, stirring well. Serve at room temperature or chilled. Serve as a dip with baked tortilla chips, or as a topping for tacos or enchiladas. Yield: 1 ¼ cups (6 servings).

## Nutrition Facts

Per serving: Calories 43 (6% calories from fat) Fat .3 g (saturated fat 0) Protein 1.5 g Carbohydrates 10 g Fiber 1 g Cholesterol 0 Sodium 106 mg.

# Breads &
# Breakfast

# Breads & Breakfast

# ATLANTIC CITY SOUR CREAM BISCUITS

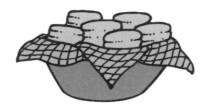

| | |
|---|---|
| 2 | cups all-purpose flour |
| 1 | teaspoon baking soda |
| 1 | teaspoon baking powder |
| ½ | teaspoon salt |
| 1 | cup non-fat sour cream |

In a medium-large bowl, blend flour, baking soda, baking powder and salt together with a whisk. Add sour cream and mix into a stiff dough. Using floured hands, turn dough out onto a floured board. Flour a rolling pin and roll dough to a ½-inch thickness. Cut biscuits with a biscuit cutter or simply with the rim of a drinking glass. Place biscuits on an ungreased cookie sheet and bake in a pre-heated 400° oven for 15-20 minutes, or until biscuits are golden brown.
Yield: 12 servings.

## Nutrition Facts

Per serving: Calories 99 (2% calories from fat) Fat .2 g (saturated fat 0) Protein 3.5 g Carbohydrate 20 g Fiber .5 g Cholesterol 1.5 mg Sodium 260 mg.

*Top toast and bagels with non-fat fruit spread, instead of butter. You will save 11 grams of fat for each tablespoon.*

## BEACH HAVEN BLUEBERRY SMOOTHIE

| | |
|---|---|
| 1 | cup fresh blueberries |
| ½ | cup orange juice |
| 1 | (8-ounce) container non-fat yogurt |
| ¼ | cup 1% milk |

Combine all in a blender and process until smooth. Yield: 1 serving.

### Nutrition Facts

Per serving: Calories 369 (4% calories from fat) Fat 2 g (saturated fat .5 g) Protein 15 g  Carbohydrates 76 g Fiber 2 g Cholesterol 6 mg Sodium 196 mg.


## BUCKWHEAT PANCAKES FROM ASBURY PARK

| | |
|---|---|
| ⅓ | cup all-purpose flour |
| 1 | cup buckwheat flour |
| 1 | tablespoon sugar |
| 1 | tablespoon baking powder |
| ¼ | teaspoon salt |
| 1 | egg |
| 1 ½ | cups skim milk |
| 2 | tablespoons canola oil |

In a large mixing bowl stir together flour, sugar, baking powder and salt. Place the egg in a separate bowl, and beat slightly with a fork. Stir in milk and oil to blend. Add egg mixture to flour mixture all at once and stir just until blended, but still lumpy.

Prepare a heated non-stick griddle or skillet with vegetable cooking spray. For each pancake, pour about ¼ cup of batter onto the cooking surface. Cook over medium heat until pancakes bubble on one side. Turn and cook until golden. Serve with maple syrup or your favorite fruit. Yield: 12 pancakes.

### Nutrition Facts

Per serving: Calories 104 (27% calories from fat) Fat 3 g (saturated fat .3 g)  Protein 4 g  Carbohydrates 16 g Fiber 1 g Cholesterol 18 mg Sodium 128 mg.

# CRESCENT CITY STUFFED FRENCH TOAST

| | |
|---|---|
| 8 | slices natural wheat or multi-grain bread |
| 4 | ounces fat-free cream cheese |
| 6 | tablespoons strawberry or raspberry jam, divided |
| 1 | tablespoon powdered sugar |
| ½ | cup egg substitute product |
| ¼ | cup 1% milk |
| 1 | tablespoon butter, divided |
| | Additional powdered sugar for sprinkling |

In a medium mixing bowl, combine cream cheese, 2 tablespoons jam and sugar; beat until smooth. Place 4 slices of bread flat on a cutting board or counter-top. Spread 4 tablespoons of jam equally on each slice. Spread the cheese mixture over the jam and top with remaining 4 slices of bread to form sandwiches. Set aside.

Beat eggs and milk together in a shallow bowl. Warm non-stick pan over medium heat. Melt ½ tablespoon butter. Dip sandwiches in egg mixture lightly, then turn to coat the other side. Cook the first two sandwiches in the melted butter until they are golden brown on both sides. Remove from pan and repeat procedure with other two sandwiches. Sprinkle sandwiches with additional powdered sugar and serve immediately. Yield: 4 servings.

## Nutrition Facts

Per serving: Calories 347 (19% calories from fat) Fat 7 g (saturated fat 1.5 g) Protein 16.5 g Carbohydrates 56 g Fiber 2 g Cholesterol 6 mg Sodium 605 mg.

*When buying bread, look for whole grain with high fiber. Two grams of fiber per slice is optimal. These breads will fill you up and not out.*

# EAST CAROLINA CORN BREAD

| | |
|---|---|
| 1 | cup self-rising cornmeal |
| 1 | (8-ounce) can cream-style corn |
| ½ | cup egg substitute |
| 1 | cup light sour cream |
| 1 | teaspoon salt |
| 2 | teaspoons sugar |

In a medium bowl, mix together corn meal, corn and egg substitute. Fold in the sour cream, salt and sugar, blending all . Pour into an 8 X 8-inch square pan that was prepared with vegetable cooking spray. Bake at 350° for 20 to 25 minutes or until cornbread is done. Yield: 9 squares.

## Nutrition Facts

Per serving: Calories 112 (21% calories from fat) Fat 3 g (saturated fat 1.5 g) Protein 4 g Carbohydrates 19 g Fiber 1.3 g Cholesterol 9 mg Sodium 562 mg.

*Use egg substitutes instead of whole eggs for baked goods. You will never know the difference.*

# ENGLISH SCONES BY THE SEA

|     |                                |
|-----|--------------------------------|
| 2   | cups all-purpose flour         |
| ¼   | cup sugar                      |
| 1   | teaspoon baking powder         |
| 2   | tablespoons margarine, melted  |
| 1   | tablespoon grated lemon rind   |
| ⅓   | cup skim milk                  |
| 1   | egg white, beaten              |
| ½   | cup chopped pecans             |

In a large bowl, mix together flour, sugar and baking powder. In a small bowl, whisk together margarine, lemon rind and skim milk. Add this mixture to the flour mix slowly until blended. Turn dough onto a baking sheet that has been sprayed with non-stick vegetable spray. Using the palm of your hand or a simple beverage glass, press or roll dough into a circle about ½-inch thick. Cut dough into wedge shapes with a small knife. Brush tops of scones with egg white and sprinkle with chopped nuts. Bake in a pre-heated 450° oven for 10-12 minutes or until scones are lightly browned. Serve warm. Yield: 10 servings.

## Nutrition Facts

Per serving: Calories 141 (23% calories from fat) Fat 4 g (saturated fat .5 g) Protein 5 g  Carbohydrates 24 g Fiber 3.5 g Cholesterol .3 mg Sodium 91 mg.

*Cutting fats in baked goods can be done by replacing butter, margarine or shortening with half the amount of corn oil, which adds a buttery flavor. Reduce baking time by a fraction.*

# FARMER'S VEGGIE OMELET

1     baking potato, cooked in it's skin
1     teaspoon canola oil
¼    cup green bell pepper, chopped
¼    cup sweet red bell pepper, chopped
1     small onion, chopped
1     cup egg beaters (equivalent to 4 eggs)
      Salt and pepper to taste

Cut baked potato into ½-inch cubes. Heat the oil in a non-stick pan. Add potatoes and sauté until potatoes are starting to brown. Remove potatoes and set aside. Spray same sauté pan with non-stick vegetable spray. Sauté the green and red bell peppers and onion until they are soft. Add the potatoes back into the pan. Pour the egg mixture over the vegetables and cook 1 to 2 minutes until the bottom of egg mixture sets. Using a wide spatula, lift one half of egg mixture and turn onto its other half. Cook another minute or two for the inside of the omelet to set. Season with salt and pepper to taste and serve. Yield: 2 servings.

## Nutrition Facts

Per serving: Calories 216 (28% calories from fat) Fat 6.5 g (saturated fat 1 g) Protein 17 g Carbohydrates 22 g Fiber 2.3 g Cholesterol 1.3 mg Sodium 518 mg.

*Replacing whole eggs with egg whites or fat-free egg substitute saves 60 calories, 5 grams of fat and 210 milligrams of cholesterol per egg.*

# GEORGIA BISCUITS JUST PEACHY

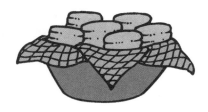

| 2 | cups all-purpose flour |
| 2 | teaspoons baking powder |
| ½ | teaspoon baking soda |
| ½ | teaspoon salt |
| 1 | cup peach-flavored yogurt at room temperature |

Pre-heat oven to 450°. Prepare a baking sheet with foil or vegetable cooking spray and set aside.

In a medium bowl, sift together flour, baking powder, baking soda and salt. Stir yogurt until creamy and add to dry ingredients. Blend mixture gently until ingredients are just moistened. Turn biscuit mixture onto a floured board. Using the palms of your hands, gently flatten dough until it is about ⅓" thick. (You may need to flour your hands to prevent sticking.) Cut biscuits using a biscuit cutter or the rim of a glass. Place on prepared baking sheet and bake for 10 to 12 minutes or until browned. Yield 18-24 biscuits (depending on size).

## Nutrition Facts

Per serving: Calories 57 (4% calories from fat) Fat .2 g (saturated fat 0) Protein 2 g Carbohydrates 12 g Fiber .4 g Cholesterol .3 mg Sodium 130 mg.

*Breakfast for a snack? Fiber-rich cereal and 1% milk fills you up on only a few calories and gives you an extra boost of bone-strengthening calcium.*

# HAMPTON BEACH HAZELNUT GRANOLA

| | |
|---|---|
| 3 | cups rolled oats |
| ½ | cup toasted wheat germ |
| ½ | cup chopped hazelnuts |
| ⅓ | cup honey |
| ⅓ | cup orange juice |
| ½ | teaspoon cinnamon |
| 1 | cup shredded coconut |

Combine oats, wheat germ and hazelnuts in a mixing bowl and set aside. In a small saucepan, stir together the honey, orange juice and cinnamon. Heat to the boiling point, then remove from heat. Add honey mixture to oat mixture, stirring to blend all .

Spray a 15x10-inch jelly roll pan with non-stick spray. Spread oat mixture evenly in pan. Bake in a 325° oven for 15 minutes or until lightly browned. Remove from oven, turn out onto a piece of foil and allow to cool. To serve, spoon granola into a bowl and top with fruit or yogurt, or serve with milk. Granola will keep for up to 2 weeks at room temperature, in an air-tight container. Yield: 10 servings (½-cup).

## Nutrition Facts

Per serving: Calories 218 (34% calories from fat) Fat 8 g (saturated fat 3 g) Protein 7 g  Carbohydrates 31 g Fiber 4.5 g Cholesterol 0 Sodium 3 mg.

*For nutritious snacking, try grain foods that will give you a fiber-boost. Air-popped pop-corn, pretzels, baked pita chips or tortilla crisps are all lower or no-fat choices.*

# MAPLE-BAKED FRENCH TOAST

| | |
|---|---|
| 1 | loaf crusty French bread |
| 2 | eggs |
| ¼ | cup egg substitute product |
| 1 | cup 1% milk |
| 2 | tablespoons sugar |
| 2 | tablespoons maple syrup |
| 1 | teaspoon vanilla |
| ¼ | teaspoon salt |
| ¼ | cup chopped walnuts (optional) |
| | Powdered confectioner's sugar for garnish |

Slice French bread into 1-inch thick slices and set aside. Prepare a baking pan by spraying it with vegetable cooking spray. Place bread into pan so that it fits with all sides touching each other and the sides of the pan. (Use two pans if needed).

In a medium mixing bowl, beat eggs, egg substitute, milk, sugar, syrup, vanilla and salt until blended. Pour egg mixture over the bread and allow it to soak into the slices. Let bread stand at least an hour, then turn it and allow all remaining egg to be absorbed into the bread. Sprinkle chopped walnuts equally over bread slices (if desired). This is a good dish to prepare the night before; simply refrigerate and remove when ready to bake.

Bake in a pre-heated 400^ oven 10 minutes, turn and bake about 4 minutes longer, or until done. To serve, sprinkle with powdered confectioner's sugar. Yield: 6 servings.

## Nutrition Facts

Per serving: Calories 351 (15% calories from fat) Fat 6 g (saturated fat 3 g) Protein 13 g  Carbohydrates 61 g Fiber 2 g Cholesterol 84 mg Sodium 720 mg.

# MARTHA'S VINEYARD OMELET SOUFFLÉ

|     |                                  |
| --- | -------------------------------- |
| 3   | egg yolks                        |
| 3   | tablespoons granulated sugar     |
| 6   | egg whites                       |
| ⅛   | teaspoon salt                    |
| 1   | teaspoon unsalted butter         |
| 1   | tablespoon confectioner's sugar  |
| 1 ½ | cups lite cherry pie filling     |

Place egg yolks and granulated sugar in a medium mixing bowl and whisk together. Beat egg whites in a separate bowl, until stiff peaks form. Fold egg whites into egg yolk mixture.

Heat a 10-inch skillet over medium-low heat and melt butter. Spread egg mixture into skillet and cook for 5 minutes, or until mixture is set on bottom. Wrap skillet handle in foil if not oven-proof. Bake egg mixture in skillet, in a pre-heated 375° oven for 5 minutes, or until it puffs. Remove from oven, dust with confectioner's sugar and serve immediately with warmed pie filling. Yield: 6 servings.

## Nutrition Facts

Per serving: Calories 149 (20% calories from fat) Fat 3 g (saturated fat 1 g) Protein 5 g  Carbohydrates 25 g Fiber 0 Cholesterol 108 mg Sodium 107 mg.

*Cutting down on sugar is easier if you use vanilla, cinnamon or nutmeg for a sweet taste without the calories.*

# NEW CASTLE CURRIED EGGS

| | |
|---|---|
| 8 | hard-cooked eggs |
| ½ | cup red onions, diced |
| ½ | cup low-fat mayonnaise |
| ½ | teaspoon curry powder |
| 1 | carrot, peeled and shredded |
| ¼ | teaspoon salt |
| ¼ | teaspoon pepper |
| | Paprika for garnishing |

Slice 6 eggs in half lengthwise, remove the yolks and place them in a small mixing bowl along with the remaining 2 whole eggs. Chop yolks and eggs and add onion, mayonnaise, curry, carrot, salt and pepper. Mix to blend all gently. Place egg white halves on a serving dish and spoon filling equally into each half. Sprinkle with paprika and serve. Yield: 6 servings.

## Nutrition Facts

Per serving: Calories 124 (50% calories from fat) Fat 7 g (saturated fat 2 g) Protein 9 g Carbohydrates 6 g Fiber .7 g Cholesterol 285 mg Sodium 348 mg.

*To keep your blood-sugar steady, you should not go longer than 4 hours without eating. The right snack will go a long way to keep your appetite in check and prevent energy lag.*

# NEW YORK BAGEL SPREAD

½   cup yogurt cheese
1   cup fat-free cream cheese, room temperature
¼   cup grated carrots
¼   cup chopped onions
¼   cup chopped celery
2   teaspoons dried parsley flakes

Place yogurt cheese and room-temperature cream cheese in a medium bowl. Using an electric mixer, blend the two cheeses. Add carrots, onions, celery and parsley flakes. Using a wooden spoon, blend gently. Refrigerate several hours for flavors to blend. This vegetable cream cheese mix keeps well in the refrigerator for two weeks. Use it with your favorite bagels or toasted bread. Yield: 12 servings.

## Nutrition Facts

Per serving: Calories 28 (10% calories from fat) Fat .3 g (saturated fat .2 g Protein 4 g   Carbohydrates 3 g Fiber .2 g Cholesterol 2 mg Sodium 116 mg.

## NO-KNEAD 2-INGREDIENT BEER BREAD

2 ⅔   cups self-rising flour
12    ounces beer at room temperature

Spay a 9x5-inch bread pan with non-stick cooking spray. Place flour into a medium mixing bowl. Add beer and stir with a wooden spoon just until mixed and flour is entirely moistened. Pour batter into prepared pan. Bake in a pre-heated 375° oven for 50 to 55 minutes until top is lightly browned and the sides have pulled away from the pan. A knife inserted into the center will come out clean when the bread is done. Cool about 5 minutes, then turn bread out onto a cooling rack. Allow to cool before slicing. Yield: 18 slices per loaf.

## Nutrition Facts

Per serving: Calories 74 (2% calories from fat) Fat .2 g (saturated fat 0) Protein 2 g Carbohydrates 15 g Fiber .5 g Cholesterol 0 Sodium 236 mg.

# OATMEAL PANCAKES FROM OREGON

1 ¼   cups oats
2     cups skim milk
1     egg
¼     cup whole wheat flour
¼     cup toasted wheat germ
¼     cup all-purpose flour
1     tablespoon baking powder
2     teaspoons sugar
2     teaspoons canola oil
½     teaspoon salt

In a medium bowl, combine the oats and the milk. Let stand for 10 minutes. Stir in the egg, flours, wheat germ, baking powder, sugar, oil and salt. Blend until all are moistened.

Heat a non-stick pan over medium heat and spray with vegetable cooking spray. Pour in ¼ cup of batter per pancake and cook, turning once, until pancakes are golden brown on both sides. Serve with syrup or your favorite fruit spread. Yield: 12 pancakes.

## Nutrition Facts

Per serving: Calories 79 (22% calories from fat) Fat 2 g (saturated fat .4 g) Protein 4 g  Carbohydrates 11 g Fiber 1 g Cholesterol 21 mg Sodium 185 mg.

# PECAN OATMEAL MUFFINS

| | |
|---|---|
| 2 | large egg whites (or equivalent egg substitute) |
| ¼ | cup maple syrup |
| 3 | tablespoons orange juice |
| 1 | cup skim milk (or 1% milk) |
| 1 | tablespoon vanilla extract |
| 1 | teaspoon ground cinnamon |
| 1 | teaspoon ground allspice |
| ¼ | teaspoon ground cloves |
| ½ | teaspoon ground nutmeg |
| 1 | tablespoon grated orange peel |
| 1 ½ | cups rolled oats |
| 1 | cup whole wheat flour |
| 1 | teaspoon baking powder |
| ¼ | cup chopped pecans |

Preheat oven to 350°. Prepare a muffin tin with vegetable cooking spray. In a large bowl, whisk egg whites until frothy. Add the maple syrup, orange juice, milk, vanilla, spices and orange peel. Mix with a wooden spoon, until well blended. Stir in the oats, flour and baking powder until all ingredients are moistened. Fold in the pecans. Fill 12 muffin cups about ⅔ full and bake for 20 minutes or until muffin tops are golden and spring back to the touch. Yield: 12 muffins.

## Nutrition Facts

Per serving: Calories 103 (18% calories from fat) Fat 2 g (saturated fat .3 g) Protein 4 g  Carbohydrates 18 g Fiber 2 g Cholesterol .5 mg Sodium 42 mg.

*Bake healthier muffins by adding a small amount of oat bran, wheat bran, ground flax or rolled oats to your recipe. To add in this extra fiber you might need to also add a few extra drops of water.*

# POACHED EGGS PORTLAND-STYLE

4    fresh eggs in the shell
2    oat bran English muffins
1    tablespoon light butter spread
½    teaspoon white vinegar
     Salt and pepper to taste

Set a large skillet filled with 8 cups of water over medium-high heat and bring to a boil. Reduce to a low simmer (small bubbles just breaking the surface of the water). While the water is heating, toast two English muffins spreading 1 tablespoon light butter spread on 4 halves.

To perfectly poach eggs, add vinegar to simmering water. Break one egg at a time into a shallow bowl and gently slip eggs into simmering water. Cook 3-5 minutes, or until the whites are firm and the yolks begins to thicken. Using a slotted spoon, remove the poached eggs and drain well. Place each egg onto a buttered English muffin half, season with salt and pepper to taste and serve immediately. Yield: 4 servings.

## Nutrition Facts

Per serving: Calories 161 (45% calories from fat) Fat 8 g (saturated fat 2.5 g) Protein 8.5 g Carbohydrates 14 g Fiber 1 g Cholesterol 218 mg Sodium 222 mg.

# RAISINY WHOLE WHEAT BRAN MUFFINS

| | |
|---|---|
| 1 | egg, beaten |
| ¾ | cup 1% milk |
| 1 | tablespoon vegetable oil |
| ¼ | cup applesauce |
| 1 ½ | cups raisin bran cereal |
| ½ | cup self-rising white flour |
| ½ | cup whole wheat flour |
| ⅓ | cup granulated sugar |
| 2 | teaspoons baking powder |
| ½ | teaspoon salt |
| ¼ | teaspoon cinnamon |

Preheat oven to 400°. Spray muffin tin with vegetable cooking spray, or line with paper liners.

In a small bowl combine egg, milk, oil and applesauce. Stir in cereal and set aside a few minutes. In a large bowl combine flours, sugar, baking powder, salt and cinnamon. Add cereal mixture all at once to flour mixture, stirring just to moisten dry ingredients. Fill muffin tins half full and bake 20 to 25 minutes or until done. Yield: 12 muffins.

NOTE: For larger muffins, use a larger size muffin tin and divide batter into 8 muffins.

## Nutrition Facts

Per serving: Calories 115 (15% calories from fat) Fat 2 g (saturated fat .4 g) Protein 3 g  Carbohydrates 23 g Fiber 2 g Cholesterol 18 mg Sodium 260 mg.

# SANIBEL ISLAND SAUSAGE AND APPLE STRATA

8    egg whites
4    whole eggs
1 ½  cup 1% milk
2    tablespoons Dijon-style mustard
⅔    teaspoon salt
½    teaspoon black pepper
6    slices multi-grain bread, cubed
8    ounces pre-cooked reduced-fat turkey sausage
½    teaspoon dried sage
2    Granny Smith apples, peeled and cubed
1 ½  cups reduced-fat Cheddar cheese, shredded

In a medium bowl, lightly beat together egg whites and whole eggs. Stir in milk, mustard, salt and pepper. Place bread cubes in a separate bowl. Remove sausage meat from casings and add to bread bowl. Stir in sage and toss to blend. Prepare a 13x9x2-inch baking dish with non-fat vegetable spray. Transfer the bread-sausage mixture to baking dish and top with apples. Slowly pour egg mixture over all. Sprinkle with cheese, cover and allow to stand 10 minutes for egg mixture to be absorbed. (Strata may be refrigerated at this point to be baked the next morning. Remove from refrigerator 30 minutes prior to baking).

Bake, covered in a pre-heated 425° oven for 10 minutes. Uncover, bake 15 minutes more, or until top is lightly browned. Allow to stand a few minutes before serving. Yield: 8 servings.

NOTE: This is a great dish for a company breakfast, as it can be prepared the night before.

## Nutrition Facts

Per serving:  Calories 204 (26% calories from fat)  Fat 6 g (saturated 2 g)  Protein 18 g  Carbohydrates 20 g  Fiber 3.5 g  Cholesterol 124 mg  Sodium 880 mg.

# SOUTHERN CORNBREAD FROM HILTON HEAD

| | |
|---|---|
| 1 | cup all-purpose flour |
| 1 | cup cornmeal |
| 2 | tablespoons sugar |
| 2 | teaspoons baking powder |
| ¼ | teaspoon salt |
| 1 | egg, lightly beaten |
| 1 | cup skim milk |
| 1 | tablespoon canola oil |

In a large mixing bowl, stir together flour, cornmeal, sugar, baking powder and salt. In a small bowl, beat together egg, milk and oil. Add egg mixture to dry, blending until dough is blended, but still lumpy.

Spray an 8"x8" baking pan with vegetable spray. Pour cornbread mix into prepared pan and bake in a pre-heated 350° oven for 30-35 minutes, or until cornbread is lightly browned and springs back gently to the touch. Serve warm. Yield: 10 servings.

## Nutrition Facts

Per serving: Calories 145 (22% calories from fat) Fat 3.5 g (saturated fat .4 g) Protein 4 g Carbohydrates 24 g Fiber 1.5 g Cholesterol 19 mg Sodium 175 mg.

# WHOLE WHEAT WAFFLES WITH WASHINGTON APPLES

½   teaspoon vegetable oil
2   cups diced Washington apples (or Granny Smith)
½   cup apple cider or juice
1   tablespoon fresh lemon juice
¾   teaspoon cinnamon, divided
1   cup whole wheat flour
1   cup cake flour
2   teaspoons baking powder
2   teaspoons baking soda
2   cups buttermilk
1   tablespoon dark molasses
3   large egg whites

Heat oil in a large non-stick skillet over medium heat. Stir in apples and cook until they turn golden, about 8-10 minutes. Add cider, lemon juice and ½ teaspoon of cinnamon. Bring mixture to a boil, remove from heat, set aside and keep warm.

Heat waffle iron while waffle mixture is being prepared as follows. Combine whole wheat flour, cake flour, baking powder, baking soda and ¼ teaspoon cinnamon in a large bowl. Stir in buttermilk and molasses until mixture is moistened. Beat egg whites in a small mixer bowl, until stiff but not dry. Fold beaten egg whites into flour mixture. Spray waffle baker surface with vegetable cooking spray and cook waffles according to manufacturer's directions. Serve with caramelized Washington apples on top. Yield: 6 servings.

## Nutrition Facts

Per serving: Calories 231 (7% calories from fat) Fat 2 g (saturated fat .6 g) Protein 10 g Carbohydrates 46 g Fiber 4 g Cholesterol 5 mg Sodium 628 mg.

# YOGURT CHEESE

16    ounces plain or flavored yogurt (that does not contain gelatin)

Place yogurt in a yogurt cheese funnel if available. Otherwise, use a colander lined with 4 layers of paper towels, place yogurt in colander and cover with more paper towels. Place draining device into a pan to drain and put it in the refrigerator. Allow to drain for 2 to 8 hours. Approximately half the yogurt will become cheese and half will become whey. Discard the whey and place the yogurt cheese in a covered container. Yogurt cheese will keep up to 4 weeks in the refrigerator. Yield: approximately 1 cup.

NOTE: Yogurt cheese is a creamy, nutritious and low-fat substitute for cream cheese, sour cream and mayonnaise. Wonderfully versatile, it will enhance and take on the flavor of most foods it is used with. It is one of the tastiest soft cheeses you will ever eat.

## Nutrition Facts

Per serving: Calories 32 (2% calories from fat) Fat .1 g (saturated fat 0) Protein 3.5 g  Carbohydrates 4.5 g Fiber 0 Cholesterol 1.3 mg Sodium 32 mg.

# Soups & Salads

# Soups & Salads

## BAJA BLACK BEAN SOUP

| | |
|---|---|
| 1 | cup dried, black beans (or 3 cans prepared black beans) |
| 2 | tablespoons olive oil |
| ½ | cup chopped carrots |
| 1 | medium-size onion, chopped |
| ½ | cup celery, chopped |
| 1 | clove garlic, crushed |
| 1 | (10-ounce) can tomatoes with green chilies |
| | Salt and pepper to taste |
| ¼ | cup dry sherry |
| ¼ | cup minced cilantro |
| | Lime slices for garnish (optional) |

Soak beans overnight (if using dried), and cook according to package directions.

Heat olive oil in a large Dutch oven. Sauté carrots, onion and celery for 5 minutes or until tender. Add garlic and sauté 1-2 minutes more. Add tomatoes, prepared beans, salt and pepper to taste. Heat to boiling; reduce heat and simmer 20 minutes, then cool. In a food processor, puree half of the cooled soup mixture. Return this to the pot and reheat. Just before serving, add sherry and cilantro. Stir gently and serve. May be served with lime slices if desired. Serves 6.

## Nutrition Facts

Per serving:  Calories 216 (17% calories from fat)  Fat 4 g (saturated fat .6 g)
Protein 11 g  Carbohydrates 33 g  Fiber 11 g  Cholesterol 0  Sodium 310 mg.

*Eating five or six "mini-meals" during the day instead of three big ones may be a good thing for some individuals.  It keeps energy levels up and prevents hunger that can lead to over- eating.  It takes discipline however, to keep these mini-meals around 250 calories.*

# BLACK BEAN & CORN CONFETTI SALAD

| | |
|---|---|
| 1 | (15-ounce) can black beans, rinsed |
| 1 | (15-ounce) can kernal corn, drained |
| 1 | large tomato, seeded and chopped |
| ⅓ | cup chopped red onion |
| ¼ | cup chopped fresh parsley |

## Marinade:

| | |
|---|---|
| 1 | tablespoon rice vinegar |
| ½ | tablespoon sesame oil |
| 1 | tablespoon lime juice |
| 1 | tablespoon canola oil |
| ½ | teaspoon chile powder |
| ¼ | teaspoon cumin |
| 2 | cloves garlic, minced |
| ½ | teaspoon salt |
| ⅛ | teaspoon pepper |

In a medium bowl, combine beans, corn, tomato, onion and parsley.

Whisk together the marinade, pour over the bean mixture and toss to blend. Refrigerate salad at least 2 hours for all flavors to blend. Yield: 6 servings.

## Nutrition Facts

Per serving:  Calories 156 (25% calories from fat)  Fat 5 g (saturated fat .5 g) Protein 6 g  Carbohydrates 26 g  Fiber 6 g  Cholesterol 0  Sodium 661

# CAPE CHARLES CRANBERRY COLESLAW

| | |
|---|---|
| 3 | cups shredded cabbage |
| 1 | cup shredded carrots |
| 1 | cup dried cranberries (3 ounces) |
| 1 | cup rice vinegar |
| ¼ | cup sugar |
| 1 | teaspoon celery seeds |
| 1 | teaspoon mustard seeds |

Combine cabbage, carrots and cranberries in a mixing bowl. Add vinegar, sugar, celery seeds and mustard seeds. Toss to blend, then refrigerate for one hour. Toss again and place in a serving dish. Yield: 6 servings.

## Nutrition Facts

Per serving: Calories 90 (4% calories from fat) Fat .4 g (saturated fat 0) Protein 1 g Carbohydrates 21 g Fiber 2.2 g Cholesterol 0 Sodium 25 mg.

*When making vinaigrette salad dressing, reverse the usual propor-
tions of 3 parts oil to 1 part vinegar. You may need to switch to a
milder vinegar such as raspberry, rice or white balsamic.*

# CARAMELIZED VIDALIA ONION SOUP

| | |
|---|---|
| 2 | tablespoons canola oil |
| 4 | pounds Vidalia onions, sliced |
| 2 | garlic cloves, minced |
| 2 | tablespoons all-purpose flour |
| 1 | (14 1/2-ounce) can low-fat chicken broth |
| 1 | cup water |
| 1 | teaspoon pepper |
| 1 | tablespoon fresh rosemary, chopped |
| 3 | (14 1/2-ounce) cans beef broth |
| 1 | cup red wine |
| 6 | French bread slices, cut in half |
| 12 | (.5-ounce) slices low-moisture mozzarella cheese |

Heat canola oil in a Dutch oven over medium heat. Reduce heat to low and cook onions and garlic 40 to 45 minutes, stirring often, until onion is caramel in color. Stir in flour and cook, stirring constantly, 2 minutes. Stir in chicken broth, water, pepper and rosemary. Stir well to remove particles from the bottom of the pan. Add the beef broth and wine and bring to a boil. Reduce heat and simmer 20 to 30 minutes, or until thickened. Top each serving with a bread slice and a piece of cheese. Yield:  12 cups

## Nutrition Facts

Per serving: Calories 187 (24% calories from fat) Fat 5 g (saturated 1.5 g) Protein 9 g  Carbohydrates 23 g  Fiber 3.3 g  Cholesterol 6 mg  Sodium 631 mg.

*Soups & Salads*

# CATCH OF THE DAY FISHERMAN'S STEW

| | |
|---|---|
| 2 | tablespoons olive oil |
| 2 | tablespoons fresh lime juice |
| 1 | pound catch of the day white fish, cut into 1-inch pieces |
| | Salt and pepper to taste |
| 1 ½ | cups chopped onion |
| 1 ½ | cups chopped bell pepper |
| 1 | chopped shallot |
| 1 | clove garlic, minced |
| ¾ | teaspoon dried crushed red pepper |
| 2 | cups fresh chopped tomatoes |
| ¾ | cup canned lite coconut milk |
| 2 | tablespoons chopped cilantro, divided |
| 1 | pound fresh medium shrimp, peeled and cleaned |

In a medium-size mixing bowl, whisk together 1 tablespoon oil and lime juice. Add fish and toss gently to coat. Sprinkle with salt and pepper to taste; let stand 15 minutes.

Heat remaining tablespoon of oil in a large pot over medium heat. Saute onions, peppers, shallot, garlic and red pepper for 5 minutes. Add tomatoes and simmer for 15 minutes. Add coconut milk, 1 tablespoon cilantro, shrimp and fish with marinade. Simmer until shrimp and fish are just opague in center, about 5 minutes. Season with salt and pepper to taste, sprinkle with remaining cilantro and serve immediately. Yield: 6 servings.

## Nutrition Facts

Per serving:  Calories 218 (28% calories from fat)  Fat 6.6 g (saturated fat 1 g) Protein 31 g Carbohydrates 8 g Fiber 1.3 g Cholesterol 170 mg Sodium 198 mg.

# CHATHAM CURRIED SPLIT PEA SOUP

| | |
|---|---|
| 1 | pound dried split green peas |
| 8 | ounces lean turkey sausage |
| 1 | tablespoon olive or canola oil |
| 1 | cup chopped celery |
| 1 | medium onion, chopped |
| 1 | cup chopped carrots |
| 1 | cup raw, chopped potatoes |
| 2 | bay leaves |
| ⅓ | cup dried cranberries |
| 1 | tablespoon curry powder |
| 1 | tablespoon dried marjoram |
| ½ | teaspoon ground pepper |
| 6 | cups water (plus more if needed) |
| | Salt to taste (optional) |

Rinse and drain the dried peas and set aside. Slice the turkey sausage into thin slices, set aside.

In a large Dutch oven, heat the oil on medium-high. Saute the chopped celery, onion, carrots and potato for a few minutes until the onion turns clear. Add the drained peas and sausage and toss to mix. Add the water, bay leaves, cranberries, curry powder, marjoram and pepper. Bring to a simmer and cook, covered, while stirring occasionally for 45 to 60 minutes. Adjust seasonings, add additional water if necessary and cook further until desired consistency. Serve with dried croutons for a great presentation. Yield: 8 servings.

## Nutrition Facts

Per serving: Calories 264 (13% calories from fat) Fat 4 g (saturated fat 1 g) Protein 18 g Carbohydrates 41 g Fiber 14 g Cholesterol 24 mg Sodium 195 mg.

# CHICKEN & LIME TORTILLA SOUP

| | |
|---|---|
| ½ | cup onion, chopped |
| 1 | clove garlic, minced |
| 1 | tablespoon margarine |
| 4 | cups fat-free chicken broth |
| 1 | chicken breast, skin removed |
| 2 | (14-ounce) cans of tomatoes with chilies |
| ¼ | cup cilantro, chopped |
| 1 | teaspoon marjoram |
| 6 | corn tortillas |
| ½ | cup reduced-fat Monterey Jack cheese, shredded |
| 1 | lime, cut into 10 slices |
| 1 | sliced avocado for garnish |

In a 3-quart saucepan, cook onion and garlic in margarine till tender and just clear. Stir in chicken broth, chicken breast, tomatoes with chilies, cilantro and marjoram. Bring to a boil; reduce heat and simmer, covered, for 35-40 minutes. Remove chicken breast to a plate to cool.

Meanwhile, stack tortillas, cut stack in half, then cut halves crosswise into 1/2-inch strips. Place strips on a cookie sheet and bake for a few minutes in a 350° oven, until they are lightly browned. Remove from oven and set aside.

When chicken is cool enough to handle, but still warm, shred chicken meat into soup. Divide tortilla strips into soup bowls and sprinkle with cheese. Place bowls in the oven briefly just until cheese melts. Remove bowls from oven carefully, and ladle the soup over the tortilla strips and cheese. Give each bowl a sprinkle of lime juice and garnish with avocado slices. Yield: 10 servings.

## Nutrition Facts

Per serving: Calories 215 (37% calories from fat) Fat 9 g (saturated fat 2.5 g) Protein 14.3 g Carbohydrates 20 g Fiber 2 g Cholesterol 25 mg Sodium 450 mg

# CHINCOTEAGUE CORN & CRAB BISQUE

| | |
|---|---|
| 4 | strips bacon |
| ½ | onion, finely chopped |
| ½ | cup celery, finely chopped |
| ½ | green pepper, finely chopped |
| ½ | red bell pepper, finely chopped |
| ½ | cup raw peeled potatoes |
| 3 | cups water |
| ¼ | teaspoon paprika |
| 1 | bay leaf |
| 3 | tablespoons flour |
| 2 | cups 1% milk, divided |
| ½ | pound crab meat, cleaned |
| 2 | cups fresh corn, cooked |
| | Parsley for garnish |

In a Dutch oven, saute the bacon until crisp; remove, cool, crumble and set aside. In the bacon drippings, saute the onion, celery and peppers until onion is soft, but not brown. Add the potatoes, water, paprika and bay leaf. Simmer until the potatoes are tender (about 35-40 minutes).

Reduce heat to the boiling point and add the flour and ½ cup of the milk. In a separate saucepan, heat crab meat, corn and the remaining milk. When warmed through, add this mixture and the bacon to the soup. Heat on low for a few minutes, but do not boil. Garnish with parsley and serve. Yield: 6 servings.

## Nutrition Facts

Per serving: Calories 216 (32% calories from fat) Fat 8 g (saturated fat 3 g) Protein 14 g Carbohydrates 24 g Fiber 2.6 g Cholesterol 45 mg Sodium 323 mg.

*If you're trying to reduce your cholesterol, switch to 1% or skim milk from whole milk. You will also cut fat and calories in half.*

# CHINESE SHRIMP WON TON SOUP

| 3 | tablespoons oil |
|---|---|
| 1 | medium onion, minced |
| 1 | clove garlic, minced |
| ½ | pound medium-size shrimp, peeled, cleaned and cooked |
| ½ | pound lite silken tofu |
| ¼ | cup dry breadcrumbs |
| 3 | tablespoons soy sauce |
| 1 | egg, lightly beaten |
| 1 | (12-ounce) package won ton wrappers |
| 4 | cups fat-free chicken broth |
| | Green onion, chopped |

Heat oil in a medium skillet and sauté onion and garlic until transparent. Meanwhile, set 6 shrimp aside for garnish and chop remaining shrimp finely. Add the chopped shrimp and the tofu to the skillet and sauté for 3 minutes. Remove mixture from skillet and place in a medium bowl. Add bread crumbs, soy sauce and beaten egg and mix together until blended.

To make won tons, fill each wrapper with about 1 teaspoon of mixture. Moisten edges of won ton with a little water, fold one corner over and press to seal. Pinch filled won tons until corners come together to seal.

Heat chicken broth in a large saucepan. When broth simmers, add won tons and gently simmer for five minutes. Ladle won ton soup into bowls, adding one whole shrimp and a teaspoon of green onion into each. Yield: 6 servings.

## Nutrition Facts

Per serving: Calories 223 (38% calories from fat) Fat 9 g (saturated fat 1 g) Protein 18 g  Carbohydrates 16 g  Fiber .7 g  Cholesterol 94 mg  Sodium 609 mg.

*Vegetable and tomato juices are a good hunger suppressant. At just 50 calories and no fat, their thickness fills you up and supplies 100% of your daily requirement for vitamin C.*

# CIOPPINO - SAN FRANCISCO STYLE

| | |
|---|---|
| 2 | tablespoons olive oil |
| 1 | medium onion, chopped |
| 3 | garlic cloves, minced |
| ½ | teaspoon dried hot red pepper flakes |
| 1 | green or red bell pepper, seeded and sliced |
| 1 | cup dry white wine |
| 1 | (28-ounce) can peeled chopped tomatoes, with liquid |
| 1 | teaspoon dried oregano |
| ½ | teaspoon thyme |
| 1 | bay leaf |
| 8 | ounces haddock, cod or halibut filet, skinned |
| 8 | ounces large raw shrimp, peeled and cleaned |
| 6 | large sea scallops |
| 12 | mussels or hard-shell clams, scrubbed clean |
| 6 | slices crusty Italian or French bread |
| 3 | tablespoons chopped fresh parsley |

Heat oil in a large heavy saucepan. Add onion, garlic, pepperflakes and bell pepper. Cook over medium heat, until onion begins to color. Add wine, tomatoes, oregano, thyme and bay leaf. Cover and simmer 30-40 minutes.

Cut fish into cubes and add to tomatoes along with shrimp, scallops and mussels. Cook over low heat, until mussels open and the seafood is done. Discard any shells that do not open. The fish should be white and flaky, the shrimp will curl and turn pink; the scallops will be firm to the touch.

Place 1 slice of crusty bread into each of 6 shallow soup bowls. Ladle soup and seafood over bread, garnish with parsley and serve. Yield: 6 servings.

## Nutrition Facts

Per serving:  Calories 367 (20% calories from fat)  Fat 8 g (saturated fat 1.5 g)
Protein 27 g  Carbohydrates 40 g  Fiber 2 g  Cholesterol 82 mg  Sodium 807 mg.

# EASTERN SHORE SHE-CRAB SOUP

| | |
|---|---|
| 1 | (6-ounce) can chopped clams with juice |
| 1 | tablespoon butter |
| 2 | shallots, finely chopped |
| ⅓ | cup sherry |
| 1 | pound lump (or other) crab meat, cartilage removed |
| 2 | teaspoons paprika |
| ¼ | teaspoon dried thyme |
| 1 | quart fat-free half & half |
| 2 | tablespoons cornstarch dissolved in ½ cup cold water |
| ⅛ | teaspoon cayenne pepper |
| | Salt and pepper to taste |
| | Fresh thyme leaves for garnish (optional) |

Drain clams reserving their liquid and place in a mini-food processor. Process briefly until they are pureed. Replace pureed clams in their liquid and add water to bring up the level to 1 ½ cups. Set aside.

Heat a large, heavy saucepan over medium heat. Melt butter and sauté chopped shallots until clear. Add sherry and simmer about 2 minutes, or until liquid is reduced by half. Add crab, pureed clams and liquid, paprika and thyme. Simmer 3 minutes. Add half & half and bring the soup to a boil. Stir in the cornstarch mixture and stir until thickened. Season with cayenne pepper, salt and pepper to taste. Serve immediately. Yield: 4 servings.

NOTE: For different preferences of soup consistency, adjust cornstarch for a thicker or thinner soup base.

## Nutrition Facts

Per serving: Calories 277 (21% calories from fat) Fat 6.3 g (saturated fat 3 g) Protein 33 g Carbohydrates 17.4 g Fiber .4 g Cholesterol 129 mg Sodium 555 mg.

# FRESH SHRIMP CAESAR SALAD

| | |
|---|---|
| 8 | cups romaine lettuce, chopped and washed |
| ¾ | pound medium shrimp, peeled and deveined |
| ¼ | cup fat-free Caesar dressing |
| 1 | tablespoon lemon juice |
| 2 | teaspoons Dijon mustard |
| 2 | garlic cloves, minced |
| 2 | tablespoons olive oil |
| ½ | teaspoon salt |
| ½ | teaspoon black pepper |
| ½ | cup fat-free Parmesan cheese |
| 2 | ounces seasoned croutons |

Place cleaned lettuce in a plastic bag and refrigerate to crisp.

Place shrimp in a medium saucepan of boiling water to cover. Simmer for about 3 minutes until cooked. Shrimp will turn pink and curl when they are done. Remove cooked shrimp from the boiling water and set aside to cool, then refrigerate. Simmer the remaining shrimp broth to reduce it and reserve 2 tablespoons for the dressing.

To make the dressing, whisk together the bottled Caesar dressing, lemon juice, mustard, garlic, olive oil, salt and pepper. Add the cooled shrimp broth to this and whisk again. The dressing may be refrigerated at this point until ready to serve.

To serve this salad, place lettuce in 8 individual salad bowls and arrange cooked shrimp on top. Pour equal amounts of dressing on each bowl, add croutons and sprinkle with Parmesan cheese. This "shrimply" delightful salad, you will not likely forget. Yield:  8 servings.

## Nutrition Facts

Per Serving:  Calories 135 (40% calories from fat)  Fat 6 g (saturated fat .5 g)
Protein 13 g Carbohydrates 7 g  Fiber 1 g  Cholesterol 66 mg  Sodium 530 mg.

# GARDEN HERB SALAD DRESSING

| | |
|---|---|
| 1 | cup plain low-fat yogurt |
| 3 | tablespoons  canola oil |
| 1 | tablespoon tarragon white wine vinegar |
| 2 | tablespoons grated white onion |
| 2 | teaspoons chopped parsley |
| ⅛ | teaspoon oregano |
| 1 | teaspoon garlic salt |
| | Dash pepper |

Place yogurt, oil, vinegar, onion, parsley, oregano, garlic salt and pepper in a blender container. Cover and blend on high speed about 2 minutes until smooth and creamy. Refrigerate about 2 hours in an air-tight container for flavors to blend. Yield:  12 servings.

## Nutrition Facts

Per serving: Calories 44 ( 76% calories from fat) Fat 4 g (saturated fat .5 g) Protein 1 g  Carbohydrates 11.5 g  Fiber 0  Cholesterol 1 mg  Sodium 14 mg.

*Not all fat-free salad dressings lack flavor.  New ones constantly come on the market.  So try them—you may like them.*

# GULF COAST SHRIMP GUMBO

| | |
|---|---|
| 2 | tablespoons olive oil |
| 2 | onions, chopped |
| 1 | green bell pepper, cored and chopped |
| 1 | stalk celery, chopped |
| 1 | clove garlic, minced |
| 2 | tablespoons flour |
| 3 | cups chicken broth or fish stock |
| 1 | (14 ½-ounce) can chopped tomatoes |
| ⅔ | cup chopped cooked ham |
| 1 | teaspoon Cajun seasoning (or ½ teaspoon cayenne) |
| 8 | ounces fresh okra, sliced |
| 1 | pound fresh medium shrimp, shelled and cleaned |
| | Lemon juice and hot pepper sauce to taste |
| 2 | cups cooked long-grain rice |

Heat oil in a large heavy saucepan. Add onions and cook until softened. Add green pepper, celery and garlic and cook, stirring frequently for 5 minutes. Add flour and stir one minute more. Stir in broth (or stock), tomatoes, ham and seasoning. Simmer, partially covered, for 30 minutes. Add okra and simmer covered, 30 minutes more. Add shrimp and cook until they turn pink and the tails curl (about 3 minutes). Do not overcook shrimp. Add lemon juice and hot pepper sauce to taste. Ladle gumbo into 4 serving bowls. Place ½ cup  cooked rice in center of each bowl and serve immediately. Yield:  4 servings.

## Nutrition Facts

Per serving:  Calories 433 (24% calories from fat)  Fat 11 g (saturated fat 2 g) Protein 42 g  Carbohydrates 39 g  Fiber 4 g  Cholesterol 185 mg  Sodium 1110 mg.

*Diets high in animal fats are heavy in saturated fat and cholesterol. Eating smaller  amounts of these fats and more "good" fats that contain omega-3 fatty acids will aid in fat  loss, reduce cholesterol and lower risk of heart disease.*

*Soups & Salads*

# HATTERAS-STYLE CLAM CHOWDER

|     |                                                              |
| --- | ------------------------------------------------------------ |
| 3   | slices bacon                                                 |
| 5   | cups water                                                   |
| 3   | white potatoes, diced                                        |
| 2   | onions, diced                                                |
| 3   | stalks celery, diced                                         |
| 2   | (6 ½-ounce) cans chopped clams (fresh may be substituted)    |
| ¼   | teaspoon thyme                                               |
| ½   | teaspoon salt                                                |
| ¼   | teaspoon pepper                                              |
|     | Parsley for garnish                                          |

Heat a large Dutch oven over medium-high. Sauté bacon until it is crispy. Remove and set aside. Add 5 cups very hot tap water to bacon drippings and bring to a boil. Add diced potatoes and cook 5 minutes. Add onions and celery; cook 10 minutes more. Add clams in their juice, bacon crumbled, thyme, salt and pepper. Simmer all for 10 to 12 minutes on low heat. Do not overcook, as clams will become tough. Garnish with parsley and serve. Yield: 6 servings.

## Nutrition Facts

Per serving: Calories 116 (51% calories from fat) Fat 6.6 g (saturated fat 4.5 g) Protein 2.7 g Carbohydrates 12 g Fiber 1.5 g Cholesterol 9.4 mg Sodium 430 mg.

# LANDLUBBER'S LEEK & POTATO SOUP

| | |
|---|---|
| 2 | tablespoons lite margarine |
| 1 | cup sliced leeks |
| ½ | cup sliced onions |
| 2 | cups peeled potatoes, diced |
| 6 | cups water |
| 4 | packets instant chicken broth mix |
| | Salt & pepper to taste |
| 1 ½ | cups evaporated skim milk |
| ¼ | cup fresh parsley, chopped |
| ¼ | cup fresh chive, chopped |

In a large saucepan, melt the margarine and cook the leeks and onions over medium heat until tender. Add the potatoes, water, chicken broth mix and simmer about 20 minutes or until potatoes are cooked. Season with salt and pepper to taste. Cool soup.

Blend the cooled soup in a blender until smooth. Return soup to the saucepan and stir in milk. Cook stirring, until heated through. Sprinkle with parsley and chives and serve. Yield:  4 servings.

## Nutrition Facts

Per serving: Calories 192 (14% calories from fat)  Fat 3 g (saturated .6 g)  Protein 8.5 g  Carbohydrates 33 g  Fiber 2.3 g  Cholesterol 0  Sodium 960 mg.

# LONG BEACH THOUSAND ISLAND DRESSING

1    cup plain low-fat yogurt
2    tablespoons chili sauce
1    hard-boiled egg, chopped
2    tablespoons pickle relish
2    tablespoon low-fat mayonnaise
1    teaspoon sugar

Combine all in a small bowl. Blend well using a wooden spoon. Refrigerate at least 2 hours in an air-tight container for flavors to blend. Yield:  12 servings.

## Nutrition Facts

Per serving:  Calories 34 (35% calories from fat)  Fat 1.3 g (saturated fat .5 g) Protein 2 g  Carbohydrates 4 g  Fiber 0  Cholesterol 22 mg  Sodium 92 mg.

# MEDITERRANEAN EGGPLANT SALAD

1    eggplant
8    Calamata olives, pitted and cut in fourths
3    large, ripe tomatoes, seeded and chopped
2    tablespoons chopped red onions
1    tablespoon fresh chopped parsley
2    tablespoons olive oil
2    tablespoons lemon juice
½    teaspoon dried oregano
     Salt and pepper to taste

Trim the stem off the eggplant and cut it into 3/4-inch cubes. Cook in boiling, salted water about 10 minutes, or until tender, but not soft. Drain, then let cool. Refrigerate for at least one hour.

When cooked eggplant is cold, place in a large salad bowl. Add olives, tomatoes, red onion and parsley. Drizzle with olive oil and lemon juice. Sprinkle with oregano and season with salt and pepper to taste. This dish goes well with crusty bread. Yield:  4 servings.

## Nutrition Facts

Per serving:  Calories 152 (52% calories from fat)  Fat 9.5 (saturated fat 1.3 g) Protein 2.5 g  Carbohydrates 17 g  Fiber 5 g  Cholesterol 0  Sodium 139 mg.

# NEW ENGLAND FISH CHOWDER

| | |
|---|---|
| 2 | slices bacon |
| ⅔ | cup chopped onion |
| ½ | cup diced celery |
| 2 | cups diced potatoes |
| 2 | cups water (more, if needed) |
| 1 | (6 ½-ounce) can clams with their juice |
| 1 | pound cod fillets (or other similar fish) |
| 1 | teaspoon salt |
| ⅛ | teaspoon pepper |
| ⅛ | teaspoon thyme |
| ⅛ | teaspoon paprika |
| 3 | cups fat-free half & half |
| ¼ | cup sliced scallions |

In a large Dutch oven, sauté bacon until crisp. Remove and set aside. Add onion and celery into drippings and cook over medium heat until soft. Add potatoes and water to cover. Simmer 8-10 minutes or until potatoes are half cooked. Drain clams, reserving clam liquid. Add clam liquid, fish, salt, pepper, thyme and paprika. Simmer until vegetables are tender, about 10-12 minutes. Gradually add half and half and clams. Simmer on low (do not boil) for 10 minutes more. Fish should flake easily with a fork. Garnish with sliced scallion and crumbled bacon bits. Yield: 6 servings.

## Nutrition Facts

Per serving: Calories 210 (23% calories from fat) Fat 5 g (saturated fat 2 g) Protein 20 g  Carbohydrates 19 g  Fiber 2 g  Cholesterol 41 mg  Sodium 636 mg.


*Keep salads light.  Pile on the greens and limit salad dressing to 1 tablespoon.  A quick way to "stretch" the dressing is to mix it with desired amount of rice vinegar.  You can get better  coverage with less fat and calories and no loss of*

*Soups & Salads*

# OYSTER STEW FROM OCRACOKE

| | |
|---|---|
| 1 | pint oysters in their liquor |
| ½ | cup sherry or dry vermouth |
| 2 | tablespoons butter |
| ½ | cup celery, diced |
| 1 | small onion, chopped |
| 1 | cup fresh mushrooms, sliced |
| ⅛ | teaspoon thyme |
| ⅛ | teaspoon garlic salt |
| | Salt and pepper to taste |
| 1 | quart fat-free half & half |
| | Fresh parsley for garnish |

Combine oysters with their liquor and sherry or vermouth; set aside. Heat a large saucepan over medium heat. Melt butter, add celery and cook for 2 minutes. Add onions and mushrooms and cook until onions are clear. Add oysters and liquid mixture, thyme, garlic salt, salt and pepper and bring to the boiling point. When the edges of the oysters begin to curl, add the half and half. Bring to the boiling point once more, being careful not to boil, as oysters will toughen. Garnish with fresh parsley and serve immediately. Yield: 4 servings.

## Nutrition Facts

Per serving: Calories 346 (37% calories from fat)  Fat 14 g (saturated fat 5 g) Protein 27.5 g  Carbohydrates 22 g  Fiber 5.5 g  Cholesterol 64 mg  Sodium 630 mg.

# PACIFIC CITY BLUE CHEESE DRESSING

| | |
|---|---|
| 1 | cup plain low-fat yogurt |
| 2 | ounces crumbled blue cheese |
| 2 | teaspoons grated onion |
| 1 | teaspoon vinegar |
| ¼ | teaspoon sugar |
| ¼ | teaspoon salt |
| | Dash pepper |

In a small bowl, stir yogurt until creamy. Blend in blue cheese, onion, vinegar, sugar, salt and pepper. Refrigerate at least 2 hours in an air-tight container for flavors to blend. Yield: 8 servings.

## Nutrition Facts

Per serving:  Calories 46 (49% calories from fat)  Fat 2.5 g (saturated fat 1.6 g) Protein 3 g  Carbohydrates 2.7 g  Fiber 0  Cholesterol 7 mg  Sodium 193 mg.

*Keep salads light.  Pile on the greens and limit salad dressing to 1 tablespoon.  A quick way to "stretch" the dressing is to mix it with desired amount of rice vinegar.  You can get better  coverage with less fat and calories and no loss of*

# POINT PLEASANT SUMMER POTATO SALAD

| | |
|---|---|
| 1 ½ | pounds red-skinned potatoes |
| 1 | teaspoon salt |
| 1 | medium bell pepper |
| 1 | stalk celery |
| ½ | medium-size onion |
| ⅓ | cup reduced-fat mayonnaise |
| ⅓ | cup fat-free sour cream |
| 2 | teaspoons Dijon mustard |
| 1 | tablespoon cider vinegar |
| | Salt and pepper to taste |

Using a vegetable brush, scrub potatoes well under running water. Chop into a large dice, leaving the skins on. Place potatoes in a large saucepan; add salt and cold water to cover. Bring to a boil over medium heat, and simmer 10 to 15 minutes or until potatoes are tender. Drain well, and set aside in a mixing bowl to cool.

While potatoes cool, chop bell pepper, celery and onions into a small dice. Add chopped vegetables to potatoes.

In a small mixing bowl, blend mayonnaise, sour cream, mustard and vinegar, whisking until well blended. When potatoes have cooled, add the mayonnaise mixture and toss gently. Season to taste with salt and pepper; refrigerate at least one hour or until ready to serve. Yield: 6 servings.

## Nutrition Facts

Per serving: Calories 120 (21% calories from fat)  Fat 3 g (saturated fat .5 g) Protein 3 g  Carbohydrates 21 g  Fiber 2 g  Cholesterol 5 mg  Sodium 910 mg.

*While mayonnaise packs a lot of fat, "lite" mayo has added sugar. For a healthier variety, mix  the high-fat version with non-fat sour cream in equal portions.  The result will be a super-creamy,  lower-fat dressing with less sugar.*

# PRETTY PASTA & VEGGIE SALAD

| | |
|---|---|
| 4 | ounces rainbow pasta twists or spirals |
| 4 | ounces bow tie pasta |
| ¾ | cup low-fat Italian salad dressing, divided |
| 1 | green bell pepper, cut into strips |
| 1 | sweet red bell pepper, cut into strips |
| 8 | raw baby carrots, julienned |
| 1 | cup raw, chopped broccoli |
| 1 | red onion, sliced into rings |
| 16 | large, pitted, black olives, sliced |
| ½ | cup fat-free Parmesan cheese |

Cook both pastas according to package directions to the "firm" stage. (Do not overcook). Run cooked pasta briefly under cold running water, to cool. Allow to drain well. Place both pastas in a large mixing bowl and toss with ¼ cup of the salad dressing. Set aside.

In a separate bowl, mix the peppers, carrots, broccoli, onions and olives together with the remaining ½ cup of the salad dressing. Toss the vegetables over the pasta and mix gently, leaving some vegetables on the top to garnish. Sprinkle the Parmesan cheese over all. Pasta salad may be served room temperature, or refrigerated to cool. Yield: 8 servings.

## Nutrition Facts

Per serving:  Calories 173 (23% calories from fat)  Fat 5 g (saturated fat .4 g) Protein 7 g Carbohydrates 28 g Fiber 2.5 g Cholesterol 3 mg Sodium 358 mg.

*Pile the veggies onto your favorite sandwich,  top a burger with lettuce and tomato,  stuff a pita with sliced onion and carrots and  add your favorites to the pizza.*

*Soups & Salads*

# SANDY HOOK SPINACH & CITRUS SALAD

| | |
|---|---|
| 6 | cups baby spinach leaves, cleaned and drained |
| 1 | cup Mandarine orange sections |
| 2 | tablespoons balsamic vinegar |
| 2 | tablespoons olive oil |
| ¼ | cup orange juice |
| ½ | teaspoon salt |
| 2 | cloves garlic, minced |
| 1 | ounce peanuts (walnuts may be substituted) |

Place the spinach in a salad bowl and arrange the Mandarin orange slices on top. Whisk together the vinegar, olive oil, orange juice, salt and garlic. Pour over salad and toss. Sprinkle nuts on top and serve. Yield:  8 servings.

## Nutrition Facts

Per serving:  Calories 74 (60% calories from fat)  Fat 5.3 g (saturated fat .7 g) Protein 2 g  Carbohydrates 6 g  Fiber 1.5 g  Cholesterol 0  Sodium 85 mg.

*Adding the olives instead of the oils to your salads saves calories and fat, but still imparts flavor.*

# THAI CHICKEN SALAD WITH PEANUT-GINGER DRESSING

| | |
|---|---|
| 4 | chicken breast halves, skinned and boned |
| | Peanut-Ginger Dressing (recipe in this chapter) |
| 3 | ounces vermicelli, uncooked |
| 4 | cups torn romaine lettuce |
| 2 | cups Chinese cabbage, thinly sliced |
| 2 | medium carrots, coarsely shredded |
| 1 | medium cucumber, thinly sliced |
| 1 | large red bell pepper, cut into strips |
| ¼ | cup chopped fresh parsley or cilantro |
| | Chopped peanuts for garnish (optional) |

Grill chicken over medium heat (350°) for about 15 minutes, or until done, turning once. Cut into thin strips, coat with 3 tablespoons dressing, toss and refrigerate at least 2 hours. Cook vermicelli according to package directions and drain. Toss with 2 tablespoons dressing and set aside until ready to serve.

Combine romaine lettuce, cabbage, carrots, cucumber and pepper, and toss to mix. Arrange salad mixture on a serving platter. Top with vermicelli, then with chicken. Garnish with peanuts, if desired, and serve with remaining Peanut-Ginger Dressing  Yield: 4 servings.

NOTE: The recipe for Peanut-Ginger Dressing follows. The nutritional analysis for this recipe does not include the dressing.

## Nutrition Facts

Per serving: Calories 342 (8% calories from fat)  Fat 3 g (saturated fat .7 g)  Protein 46 g  Carbohydrates 31.5 g  Fiber 4 g  Cholesterol 99 mg  Sodium 156 mg.

# THAI PEANUT-GINGER DRESSING

½    cup rice wine vinegar
2    cloves garlic
⅓    cup creamy peanut butter
¼    cup lime juice
¼    cup chopped fresh cilantro
2    tablespoons apple cider vinegar
1    tablespoon honey
1    tablespoon molasses
1    tablespoon hot sauce
2    teaspoons peeled, grated gingerroot
2    teaspoons soy sauce

Combine all in a container or electric blender; process until smooth. Yield: 1 ½ cups (or 12 2-tablespoon servings).

## Nutrition Facts

Per serving: Calories 65 (46% calories from fat) Fat 3.5 g (saturated fat .5 g) Protein 2 g Carbohydrates 7 g Fiber .5 g Cholesterol 0 Sodium 200 mg.

*Coconut extract is a good substitute for high-fat coconut milk in Thai and Indian dishes. Just add a few drops into low-fat milk to save 400 calories and 44 grams of fat per cup.*

# TORTELLINI, SPINACH & WHITE BEAN SOUP

| | |
|---|---|
| 4 | cups low-fat chicken broth |
| 1 | (8-ounce) package cheese tortellini |
| 2 | fresh tomatoes, chopped |
| 1 | (15-ounce) can white beans (any variety) |
| 2 | tablespoons shredded fresh basil |
| 1 | cup torn fresh spinach |
| 2 | tablespoons balsamic vinegar |
| ¼ | teaspoon salt |
| ⅓ | cup grated Parmesan cheese |
| | Freshly ground pepper to taste |

Place chicken broth in a large saucepan or Dutch oven and bring to a boil. Add the tomatoes and tortellini and cook for exactly half of the cooking time allowed on the package directions. Add the beans, basil and spinach. Bring to a simmer and cook 4 to 5 minutes, just until the spinach is tender and tortellini is still firm. Remove from heat and stir in balsamic vinegar and salt. Sprinkle with Parmesan cheese and fresh pepper and serve. Yield: 6 servings.

## Nutrition Facts

Per serving: Calories 237 (19% calories from fat) Fat 5 g (saturated fat 2.7 g) Protein 15.4 g Carbohydrates 30.5 g Fiber 4 g Cholesterol 18 mg Sodium 596 mg.

*Making soups, stews and sauces a day ahead and refrigerating them, allows the fat to solidify on top when cooled. The fat can then be skimmed off before reheating.*

# Vegetables &
# Casseroles

# Vegetables & Casseroles

# AMELIA ISLAND ARTICHOKE HEARTS IN LEMON BUTTER

| | |
|---|---|
| 2 | (9-ounce) packages frozen artichoke hearts |
| 1 | tablespoon butter |
| ½ | cup minced onion |
| 1 | garlic clove, minced |
| ¾ | cup non-fat chicken broth |
| 3 | tablespoons lemon juice |
| 1 ½ | teaspoons salt |
| 1 | teaspoon oregano |
| ¼ | teaspoon grated lemon rind |

Cook artichoke hearts according to directions on the package. Set aside. Heat a medium saucepan and spray with vegetable cooking spray. Melt butter and sauté the onion and garlic until they are transparent. Add broth, lemon juice, salt, oregano and lemon rind. Simmer 10 minutes, then add artichoke hearts. Heat through and serve. Yield: 8 servings.

## Nutrition Facts

Per serving:  Calories 50 (25% calories from fat)  Fat 1.5 g (saturated fat 1 g)
Protein 3 g Carbohydrates 8 g  Fiber 3.5 g  Cholesterol 4 mg  Sodium 527 mg.

# BEAUFORT BAKED BEAN CASSEROLE

½    cup firmly packed brown sugar
⅓    cup prepared mustard
¼    cup molasses
3    (15-ounce) cans pinto beans, drained
1    green bell pepper, chopped
1    sweet red pepper, chopped
1    medium-size onion, diced

In a medium-size bowl, mix together brown sugar, mustard and molasses until smooth. Stir brown sugar mixture with beans, green and red peppers and onion. Pour bean mixture into a two-quart baking dish. Bake, uncovered in a pre-heated 350° oven for about 1 ½ hours, or until slightly thickened. May be served hot or at room temperature. Yield: 8 servings.

## Nutrition Facts

Per serving 203 (7% calories from fat)  Fat 1.5 (saturated fat .3 g)  Protein 7 g
Carbohydrates 43 g  Fiber 6.5 g  Cholesterol 0  Sodium 495 mg.

*To boost protein and fiber in salads, keep on hand a selection of assorted canned beans. Beans added to salad make a quick, complete and nutritious meal.*

# BEETS 'N' GREENS

| | |
|---|---|
| 1 | ham hock |
| 4 | cups water |
| ¼ | pound ham, cut in cubes |
| 1 | 2-pound bunch collard greens, washed, trimmed and chopped (about 8 cups) |
| 1 | 2-pound bunch turnip greens, washed, trimmed and chopped (about 6 cups) |
| 3 | medium-size fresh beets, peeled and sliced |
| ½ | teaspoon sugar |
| ½ | teaspoon hot pepper vinegar |
| ½ | teaspoon salt |
| ¼ | teaspoon pepper |

Place ham hock in a large Dutch oven, add water and bring to a boil over high heat. Cover, reduce heat and simmer 30 minutes. Remove and discard ham hock.

Add cubed ham and cook for 5 minutes. Add collards, cook covered for 15 minutes, then add turnip greens, beets, sugar and salt. Cook, stirring occasionally, an additional 15 minutes, or until the vegetables are tender. Season with salt and pepper to taste, add hot vinegar and toss to blend . Yield: 4 servings.

## Nutrition Facts

Per serving:  Calories 132 (13% calories from fat)  Fat 2 g (saturated fat .5 g) Protein 14 g  Carbohydrates 16 g  Fiber 6 g  Cholesterol 8 mg  Sodium 1703 mg.

*To boost your intake of vegetables, stir some into your soup to make it thicker and healthier.*

# CAJUN RED POTATO BAKE

| | |
|---|---|
| 1 | pound baking potatoes |
| 2 | teaspoons canola oil |
| 1 | tablespoon Cajun seasoning |

Scrub potatoes well with a vegetable scrubbing brush. Cut each potato into wedges, leaving the skin on. In a large bowl, blend the potatoes and the oil. Add the seasoning and toss to coat well. Spray a baking dish with vegetable cooking oil to prevent sticking and add the seasoned potato wedges. Bake in a pre-heated 400° oven for 25-30 minutes or until done. Serves 6.

## Nutrition Facts

Per serving:  Calories 76 (19% calories from fat)  Fat 1.5 g (saturated fat .1 g) Protein 2 g  Carbohydrates 14 g  Fiber 1.3 g  Cholesterol 0  Sodium 242 mg.

*One medium baked potato has 120 calories, no fat and 2 grams of fiber. A real filler-upper and a good diet food without the high-fat toppings of butter and sour cream. Try a mixture of salsa and sour cream or sprinkle with lemon juice, salt and pepper instead, for something healthier.*

# CALIFORNIA AVOCADOS STUFFED
# WITH CRAB MEAT

| | |
|---|---|
| 1 | pound fresh crab meat, cartilage removed |
| 1 | tablespoon butter |
| 2 | tablespoons flour |
| 1 | cup 1% milk |
| ¼ | teaspoon salt |
| ⅛ | teaspoon pepper |
| ¼ | teaspoon Worcestershire sauce |
| 2 | tablespoons chopped pimento |
| 2 | tablespoons chopped olives |
| 3 | ripe California avocados |
| ¼ | cup fat-free Parmesan cheese |

Check over crab meat to insure that all cartilage has been removed. In a medium-size saucepan, melt butter and blend in flour. Gradually add milk and cook until thick and smooth, stirring constantly. Add salt, pepper, Worcestershire sauce, pimento, olives and crab meat. Cut avocados in half; remove seeds. Fill centers with crab mixture and sprinkle cheese over top of each avocado half. Place in a non-stick baking pan, or one that has been sprayed with nonstick cooking spray. Bake in a pre-heated 350° oven for 20 to 25 minutes, or until brown. Serves 6.

## Nutrition Facts

Per serving: Calories 234 (50% calories from fat)  Fat 13.5 g (saturated fat 3 g) Protein 21 g  Carbohydrates 10 g  Fiber 3.5 g  Cholesterol 60 mg  Sodium 515 mg.

*Flavorful Parmesan cheese sprinkled on pasta or salad packs a lot of punch. To halve the fat and still have the flavor, blend it with it's fat-free version in equal portions.*

# CHEESY MACARONI AND CAULIFLOWER BAKE

| | |
|---|---|
| 2 | cups cauliflower pieces |
| 8 | ounces elbow macaroni |
| 1 | tablespoon butter or margarine |
| 1 | large onion, chopped |
| 2 | cups 1% milk |
| 2 | tablespoons all-purpose flour |
| ½ | teaspoon salt |
| ¼ | teaspoon black pepper |
| 6 | ounces low-fat sharp Cheddar cheese, shredded |
| 2 | cups 1% cottage cheese |
| 2 | teaspoons Dijon mustard |
| ¼ | cup grated Parmesan cheese |
| ¼ | cup dry bread crumbs |

Cook cauliflower in boiling, salted water until firm and set aside. In a separate large saucepan, cook the macaroni according to package directions until al dente (firm).

At the same time, melt the butter in a non-stick saucepan. Add the onion and cook until soft, about 5 minutes. Combine ½ cup of the milk and flour in a blender and process until blended. Stir the flour mixture into the onions and add the salt, pepper and remaining 1 ½ cups milk. Cook over medium heat, stirring often, until slightly thickened (about 10-12 minutes). Remove from heat and stir in the Cheddar cheese.

Puree the cottage cheese and mustard in the blender until smooth. Gradually stir the cottage cheese mixture into the Cheddar cheese. Drain the macaroni when cooked, and add the cheese mixture and cooked cauliflower, stirring gently to blend all. Pour entire mixture into a prepared baking dish sprayed with vegetable cooking spray. Combine the Parmesan cheese with the bread crumbs and sprinkle over casserole. Bake in a pre-heated 375° oven for 30-40 minutes, or until done. Yield: 8 servings.

## Nutrition Facts

Per serving: Calories 266 (21% calories from fat) Fat 6 g (saturated fat 3 g) Protein 21 g  Carbohydrates 32 g  Fiber 2.2 g  Cholesterol 13 mg  Sodium 677 mg.

## CORN GRILLED-IN-THE-HUSK

| | |
|---|---|
| 6 | ears fresh corn, husks on |
| 1 | teaspoon canola oil |
| 1 | teaspoon salt (optional) |

Soak the corn cobs in their husks in hot tap water for 20 minutes. Drain them thoroughly. Tear off all but the last two layers of outer leaves. Leaving these attached to the cob, pull them back and brush kernels with oil. Cook over a hot barbecue for 40 minutes, turning and brushing with oil once or twice. Serve hot off the grill, salting just before serving, if desired. Yield: 6 ears.

### Nutrition Facts

Per serving: Calories 91 (22% calories from fat) Fat 2.5 g (saturated fat .25 g) Protein 3 g Carbohydrates 17 g Fiber 2.5 g Cholesterol 0 Sodium 401 mg.

## GINGERED BROCCOLI WITH TOASTED SESAME SEEDS

| | |
|---|---|
| 2 | teaspoons sesame seeds |
| 4 | cups broccoli flowerets |
| 1 | small sweet red pepper, cut into 1x¼-inch strips |
| 1 | tablespoon peeled, minced gingerroot |
| 1 | clove garlic, minced |
| ½ | teaspoon dark sesame oil |
| ¼ | teaspoon salt |

Heat a small nonstick skillet over medium heat. Add sesame seeds and cook, stirring constantly, 1 to 2 minutes or until seeds are golden. Remove from heat.
Steam broccoli in a small amount of water until firm (about 3-4 minutes). Add red pepper, cook 30 seconds and drain broccoli, reserving cooking liquid.
Coat a large nonstick skillet with cooking spray; place over medium heat until hot. Add gingerroot and garlic; sauté 30 seconds. Add ⅓ cup reserved cooking liquid and bring to a boil. Add broccoli mixture, sesame oil and salt and toss together. Transfer to a serving platter, sprinkle with toasted sesame seeds and serve. Yield: 4 servings.

### Nutrition Facts

Per serving: Calories 39 (23% calories from fat) Fat 1 g (saturated fat .1g) Protein 1.7 g Carbohydrates 6 g Fiber 3 g Cholesterol 0 Sodium 166 mg.

# GRAYLAND BEACH GRILLED ASPARAGUS

1 pound fresh asparagus
¼ cup low-calorie Italian salad dressing
Salt & pepper (optional)

Wash asparagus gently and trim down tough, woody stems. Place aspara-gus in a bowl and using half of the dressing, marinate for at least one hour.

In the meantime, preheat grill to medium. When ready to cook, place asparagus in a grilling basket (or on a vegetable grid) and place this on the grill. Cook asparagus 4-5 minutes, then turn and cook 2-3 minutes more or until done. Asparagus should be firm when cooked. Remove from heat and brush on remaining dressing. Season with salt and pepper if desired before serving. Yield: 4 servings.

## Nutrition Facts

Per serving: Calories 46 (29% calories from fat) Fat 1.5 g (saturated fat .2 g Protein 2.5 g Carbohydrates 5.6 g Fiber 2.5 g Cholesterol 1 mg Sodium 118 mg.

*Next time you grill, throw on a few bell peppers, onions, tomatoes, zucchini or eggplant slices marinated with a tablespoon of balsamic vinegar for a dazzling and wonderful treat.*

# GREEN BEANS IN TOMATO VINAIGRETTE

| | |
|---|---|
| 1 ½ | cups fresh tomatoes, seeded and chopped |
| ¼ | cup green onions, finely chopped |
| 1 | tablespoon fresh basil |
| 1 | teaspoon minced fresh thyme (or ½ teaspoon dry) |
| ½ | teaspoon dried marjoram |
| ½ | teaspoon dried oregano |
| ⅛ | teaspoon freshly ground pepper |
| 3 | tablespoons red wine vinegar |
| 2 | tablespoons balsamic vinegar |
| 2 | tablespoons olive oil |
| ½ | teaspoon sugar |
| 1 | pound fresh green beans |

In a medium mixing bowl, combine the tomatoes, onions, basil, thyme, marjoram and pepper. Toss to mix. In a small container, combine vinegars, oil and sugar. Using a wire whisk, stir well. Pour the vinegar mixture over the tomato mixture and toss gently. Let stand at room temperature while the beans are prepared.

Wash beans, trim ends and remove strings. Cut into 2-inch pieces and arrange in a vegetable steamer over boiling water. Cover and steam about 5 minutes or until beans are crisp-tender, then drain. Place in a serving bowl, and pour tomato vinaigrette over all; toss gently and serve. Yield: 6 servings.

NOTE: This recipes is good served chilled.

### Nutrition Facts

Per serving:  Calories 81 (49% calories from fat)  Fat 4.7 g (saturated fat .7 g) Protein 2 g  Carbohydrates 9.5 g  Fiber 3.3 g  Cholesterol 0  Sodium 12 mg.

*Store most vegetables in the refrigerator. Exposure to heat and sun can cause loss of certain nutrients.*

# GRILLED TOMATO, BELL PEPPER AND PORTOBELLO SALAD

| | |
|---|---|
| 3 | portobello mushrooms |
| 3 | medium-size green bell peppers |
| 3 | fresh tomatoes |
| 3 | green onions, chopped |
| 2 | garlic cloves, minced |
| 1 | teaspoon ground cumin |
| ½ | teaspoon salt |
| ½ | teaspoon pepper |
| 2 | tablespoons chopped fresh parsley |
| 2 | tablespoons olive oil |
| 2 | tablespoons red wine vinegar |
| 1 | tablespoon lemon juice |
| | Lemon slices and green onions for garnish |

Grill mushrooms, bell peppers and tomatoes, with the grill lid down, over medium-high heat (350°-400°) turning occasionally, until peppers and tomatoes looked blistered and mushrooms blacken. This should take about 10 minutes. Place peppers in a zip-lock bag, seal and let stand 10 minutes to loosen skins. Peel peppers, remove and discard seeds. Peel tomatoes and chop. Chop the peppers and mushrooms. Stir together the grilled chopped vegetables, green onions, garlic, cumin, salt and pepper, parsley, olive oil, vinegar and lemon juice. Toss gently to blend all . Arrange on a serving dish and garnish. Serve this dish at room temperature or refrigerated, as desired. Yield: 6 servings.

## Nutrition Facts

Per serving:  Calories 84 (47% calories from fat)  Fat 4.8 g (saturated fat .6 g) Protein 2 g  Carbohydrates 10 g  Fiber 3.3 g  Cholesterol 0  Sodium 206 mg.

# GULFPORT GARLIC MASHED POTATOES

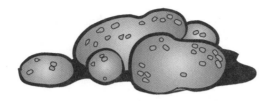

| | |
|---|---|
| 4 | cups raw potatoes, peeled and chopped |
| 1 | cup fat-free sour cream |
| ¼ | cup 1% milk |
| 1 | whole bulb of roasted garlic cloves (recipe in this section) or 2 cloves minced garlic |
| 1 | tablespoon margarine |
| | Salt and pepper to taste |

Cook potatoes until soft, remove from heat and drain, reserving 1 cup of potato water. Place cooked potatoes in a large bowl and using an electric mixer on low, blend in sour cream, milk, garlic, salt and pepper. Increase speed to medium, then to high as potatoes become creamier. Add potato water to improve the texture of the mashed potatoes as you desire. Yield: 6 servings.

## Nutrition Facts

Per serving: Calories 156 (12% calories from fat) Fat 2 g (saturated .8 g) Protein 5.5 g Carbohydrates 29 g Fiber 1.7 g Cholesterol 7 mg Sodium 452 mg.

*Use your blender to mix low-fat milk and fresh fruit into a smooth, creamy, low-fat drink.*

# LIMA BEAN CASSEROLE DEL MAR

| | |
|---|---|
| 2 | cups fresh (or frozen) shelled baby lima beans |
| 3 | slices bacon |
| 2 | tablespoons flour |
| 3 | tablespoons brown sugar |
| 1 ½ | teaspoon salt |
| ¼ | teaspoon pepper |
| 1 ½ | tablespoons dry mustard |
| 1 ½ | tablespoons lemon juice |
| ½ | cup dry bread crumbs |
| 1 | tablespoons butter, melted |
| ¼ | cup (1 ounce) medium Cheddar cheese, shredded |

Cook lima beans in boiling water for 20 minutes, or until tender. Drain and reserve 1 cup cooking liquid (add water to make 1 cup if necessary). Place lima beans into an 8-inch square baking dish that has been sprayed with nonstick cooking spray; set aside.

Heat a large skillet over medium-high heat and cook bacon until crisp. Remove bacon, reserving 2 tablespoons of drippings and drain on paper towels. Heat the bacon drippings, add flour and stir until smooth. Cook for 1 minute over medium heat, stirring constantly, until mixture is thickened. Stir in brown sugar, salt, pepper, mustard and lemon juice; pour sauce over beans. Combine breadcrumbs and butter and sprinkle over the top.

Bake in a pre-heated 350° oven for 25 minutes; sprinkle with cheese and bake for 5 minutes more, or until cheese melts. Sprinkle with crumbled bacon and serve. Yield: 6 servings.

## Nutrition Facts

Per serving: Calories 237 (39% calories from fat)  Fat 10 g (saturated fat 4 g) Protein 8 g  Carbohydrates 28 g  Fiber 4 g  Cholesterol 14 mg  Sodium 791 mg.

# MYRTLE BEACH VEGETABLE BAKE

| | |
|---|---|
| 2 | cups zucchini, thinly sliced |
| 1 | large white onion, cut into rings |
| 3 | ripe tomatoes, cut into slices |
| ½ | cup fat-free Parmesan cheese |
| 2 | teaspoons olive oil |
| | Salt & pepper to taste |

Prepare an 11x 7-inch baking dish with vegetable cooking spray. Layer half of the zucchini slices on the bottom, then half the onion rings, tomatoes and Parmesan cheese. Repeat these layers once more, ending with tomato slices. Drizzle olive oil over the top, season with salt and pepper and sprinkle with remaining Parmesan cheese. Bake in a pre-heated 400° oven for 20 to 30 minutes. Serve hot. Yield: 6 servings.

### Nutrition Facts

Per serving: Calories 61 (25% calories from fat) Fat 2 g (saturated fat .3 g) Protein 5 g  Carobhydrates 8 g  Fiber 2 g  Cholesterol 2 mg  Sodium 332 mg.

# OVEN-ROASTED RED POTATOES

| | |
|---|---|
| 1 | pound small red potatoes, halved |
| ¼ | cup fresh lemon juice |
| 1 | tablespoon olive oil |
| ½ | teaspoon salt |
| ¼ | teaspoon pepper |

Place potatoes in a plastic bag and add the lemon juice, olive oil, salt and pepper. Close bag and shake to blend all . Pour potatoes and marinade into a 13x9x2-inch casserole or baking pan. Bake in a pre-heated 350° oven for 30-40 minutes, turning potatoes to baste, until they are done. Yield: 4 servings.

### Nutrition Facts

Per serving: Calories 124 (24% calories from fat) Fat 3.5 g (saturated .5 g) Protein 2.5 g  Carbohydrates 22 g  Fiber 2 g  Cholesterol 0  Sodium 298 mg.

# PASCAGOULA PURPLE CABBAGE WITH BACON

|   |   |
|---|---|
| 2 | slices bacon |
| 1 | small head purple cabbage, shredded (about 1 ½ pounds) |
| ½ | cup dry red wine |
|   | Salt and freshly ground pepper to taste |
| 2 | green onions, sliced |

Heat a large, heavy skillet over medium-high heat. Cook bacon until crisp, about 7 minutes. Remove and drain on paper towels.

Stir the cabbage into the bacon drippings and cook, tossing, for 2 minutes. Stir in the wine and season with salt and pepper as desired. Simmer over medium heat, tossing from time to time, until the liquid is evaporated and the cabbage is tender, about 15 minutes. Do not overcook. Crumble the bacon and stir into the cabbage. Serve hot, garnished with the green onion slices. Yield: 6 servings.

## Nutrition Facts

Per serving: Calories 86 (46% calories from fat) Fat 4.7 g (saturated fat 1.7 g) Protein 2.5 g Carbohydrates 7 g Fiber 2.7 g Cholesterol 5 mg Sodium 77 mg.

*Fresh vegetables have a wide variety of colors, textures and tastes. Few contain fat or cholesterol and many contain cancer-fighting agents like Vitamin A and beta-carotene. So—eat your veggies!*

# RATATOUILLE ALFREDO

| | |
|---|---|
| 2 | teaspoons canola oil |
| 1 | large onion, chopped |
| 1 | medium eggplant |
| 1 | red bell pepper, chopped |
| 1 | yellow bell pepper, chopped |
| 2 | cloves garlic, finely chopped |
| | Salt and pepper to taste |
| 2 | medium tomatoes, seeded and chopped |
| ½ | cup chopped fresh parsley |
| 1 | cup low-fat cottage cheese |
| ¼ | cup non-fat plain yogurt |
| 2 | egg whites |
| ¼ | cup all-purpose flour |
| ½ | cup fat-free Parmesan cheese |

Prepare eggplant, by cutting into cubes, leaving the skin on. Place eggplant cubes in a colander, sprinkle with salt, then water and let drain in a sink for about 30 minutes to eliminate any bitter taste. Prepare a 7" x 11" pan with vegetable spray.

Heat canola oil to medium in a large non-stick skillet. Add onion and saute 2 minutes, then add eggplant, peppers and garlic. Season with salt and pepper and saute for about 5 minutes or until eggplant is tender. Stir in tomatoes and half of the parsley and cook for another 2 to 3 minutes. Remove skillet from heat and allow vegetables to sit.

Meanwhile, place cottage cheese, yogurt, egg whites, baking powder and half of the Parmesan cheese in a blender. Process until mixture is smooth. Place half of the vegetables in the prepared baking pan, pour the cottage cheese mixture on top and finish with the remaining vegetables. Sprinkle with the remaining cheese and parsley, and bake in a 350° pre-heated oven 30 to 40 minutes or until just lightly browned. Yield: 6 servings.

## Nutrition Facts

Per serving: Calories 149 (14% calories from fat) Fat 2.4 g (saturated fat .5 g) Protein 13 g Carbohydrates 20 g Fiber 3.5 g Cholesterol 5 mg Sodium 423 mg.

# REHOBETH BEACH ROASTED ASPARAGUS

| | |
|---|---|
| 2 | pounds fresh asparagus |
| 2 | teaspoons toasted sesame oil |
| 2 | teaspoons virgin olive oil |
| ¼ | teaspoon salt |

### Vinaigrette:

| | |
|---|---|
| ⅓ | cup soy sauce |
| 3 | tablespoons rice vinegar |
| ½ | tablespoon toasted sesame oil |
| 1 | tablespoon sugar |
| 2 | tablespoons minced parsley |

Trim off the tough, woody ends of the asparagus, rinse and drain well. Spread asparagus spears on an ungreased cookie sheet. Brush with combined oils and sprinkle with salt. Roast in a pre-heated 375° oven for 10-12 minutes or just until crisp-tender. Arrange spears on a serving plate. Mix soy sauce, rice vinegar, sesame oil and sugar together and drizzle over the asparagus. Sprinkle with parsley and serve warm or at room-temperature. Yield: 6-8 servings.

### Nutrition Facts

Per serving: Calories 66 (41% calories from fat) Fat 3.4 g (saturated fat .5 g) Protein 3 g Carbohydrates 7.7 g Fiber 2.5 g Cholesterol 0 Sodium 430 mg.

# ROASTED RED PEPPERS

| | |
|---|---|
| 6 | sweet red bell peppers |

Wash peppers and drain on paper towels. Remove and discard stems, seeds, and ribs. Place in a pre-heated broiler oven or on a grill 2 inches from heat source, skin side down. Cook, turning until peppers are well-charred or blackened on all sides (12-15 minutes). Place the charred peppers in a paper bag, close tightly and let stand for 10 minutes or more. Peel peppers and cut them into strips or pieces as desired. These peppers can be used in salads, pasta dishes or as part of an appetizer. Yield: 6 roasted peppers.

### Nutrition Facts

Per serving: Calories 44 (6% calories from fat) Fat .3 g (saturated fat 0) Protein 1.5 g Carbohydrates 10.5 g Fiber 3.3 g Cholesterol 0 Sodium 3 mg.

# SANTA BARBARA SPINACH ENCHILADAS

| | |
|---|---|
| 1 | tablespoon butter or margarine |
| 2 | green onions, chopped |
| 1 | garlic clove, minced |
| 1 | (10-ounce) package frozen chopped spinach, thawed and drained |
| 1 | cup 1% cottage cheese |
| ½ | cup fat-free sour cream |
| 4 | ounces shredded Monterey Jack cheese |
| 4 | ounces fat-free shredded Cheddar cheese |
| 10 | corn tortillas |
| 1 | 10-ounce can mild enchilada sauce |

Melt butter or margarine in a saucepan over moderate heat. Sauté the green onions and garlic for 2 minutes. Add spinach and cook 3-4 minutes, stirring occasionally. Remove from heat and set aside.

Pre-heat oven to 375°. Using a food processor or a blender, puree the cottage cheese and sour cream. In a medium bowl, add the cheese mixture, spinach mixture and half of the shredded cheeses, stirring to blend to form the enchilada filling.

Heat an ungreased skillet or griddle over medium-high heat. Heat tortillas, one at a time, about 15 seconds, turning frequently. Spoon ¼ cup filling down the center of each tortilla, roll it up and place seam-side down in a 13X9-inch baking dish. Top with enchilada sauce and remaining shredded cheeses. Bake for 15-20 minutes until bubbly. Yield: 10 enchiladas.

## Nutrition Facts

Per serving:  Calories 192 (28% calories from fat)  Fat 6 g (saturated fat 2.5 g)
Protein 13 g  Carbohydrates 21 g  Fiber 2 g  Cholesterol 13 mg  Sodium 748 mg.

*Check labels (especially on commercially-baked goods) for hydrogenated fats and oils. They are unhealthy and unfortunately, this is not yet emphasized on our current labels. Avoid foods that contain them.*

# SOUTHAMPTON SPINACH, ZUCCHINI AND POTATO PANCAKES

| | |
|---|---|
| 1 | pound zucchini, shredded |
| 1 | (10-ounce) package frozen chopped spinach, thawed and dried |
| 1 | large baking potato, shredded |
| ⅓ | cup minced onion |
| ¼ | cup all-purpose flour |
| 1 | large egg |
| ¾ | teaspoon salt |
| ½ | teaspoon pepper |
| 1 | tablespoon canola oil |

Place shredded zucchini, chopped spinach, shredded potato and minced onion into a large mixing bowl. Add flour, egg, salt and pepper: toss gently to blend all ingredients. Heat a non-stick skillet over medium heat and add 1 teaspoon of oil at a time, tipping pan to coat the bottom. Drop a heaping tablespoonful of vegetable mixture for each pancake and sauté on one side only, flattening tops with a spoon and cooking until bottoms set. Remove pancakes and place them cooked side down on foil-lined cookie sheets.

Cook remaining pancakes using 1 teaspoon oil with each batch. When all pancakes are cooked on one side, place the cookie sheets in a pre-heated 350° oven to cook for 5-7 minutes, or until the tops are brown. Yield: 25-30 pancakes or enough for 8 servings (3 pancakes per serving).

NOTE: These vegetable pancakes go well with applesauce, horseradish or reduced-fat sour cream.

## Nutrition Facts

Per serving:  Calories 83 (28% calories from fat)  Fat 2.8 g (saturated fat .4 g) Protein 4 g  Carbohydrates 12 g  Fiber 2.3 g  Cholesterol 26 mg  Sodium 328 mg.

# SOUTHPORT SAUTEED SPINACH AND SWEET PEPPERS

| | |
|---|---|
| 1 | teaspoon canola oil |
| 1 | medium onion, diced |
| 1 | medium sweet red or yellow pepper, chopped |
| 2 | cloves garlic, minced |
| 4 | ounces fresh spinach leaves, trimmed and chopped |
| | Salt and pepper to taste |

Heat a nonstick skillet over medium-high heat. Add oil and sauté onion, peppers and garlic until peppers are soft and onions are translucent. Add spinach, salt and pepper to taste and sauté one minute more. Serve warm. Yield: 4 servings.

## Nutrition Facts

Per serving:  Calories 104 (15% calories from fat)  Fat 1.8 g (satuated fat .2 g)
Protein 3.6 g  Carbohydrates 19 g  Fiber 1.5 g  Cholesterol 21 mg  Sodium 154 mg.

*Keep cut-up vegetables such as carrots, celery, bell peppers, snap peas and whole cherry tomatoes in a plastic bag in the refrigerator for quick hunger aids.*

# STRING BEANS WITH FRESH TOMATOES

½   pound fresh green beans
2   teaspoons olive oil
¼   cup red onion, chopped
2   garlic cloves, minced
2   fresh large tomatoes, peeled and chopped or
     1 (14 ½-ounce) can of chopped peeled tomatoes
⅓   cup white wine
½   teaspoon sugar
½   teaspoon salt
¼   teaspoon black pepper
½   teaspoon oregano
2   tablespoons fresh parsley, chopped
2   basil leaves

Wash and trim ends of green beans. Using a medium saucepan, par-boil beans for 5 minutes in ¾ cup of water. Remove pan from heat, drain and set aside.

Heat olive oil in a large saucepan. Sauté onion for 1 minute. Add garlic and sauté one minute more. Add tomatoes and white wine; bring tomato mixture to a boil. Lower heat to medium and add sugar, salt and pepper, oregano, parsley and basil leaves. Cook at a slow boil, stirring occasionally until tomatoes soften (about 20 minutes). Stir in green beans, reserving cooking liquid. Simmer until beans are cooked to desired texture. You may like them tender or crisp. Use the vegetable cooking liquid to add to the pot, if needed. Yield: 4 servings.

NOTE: You may use the same recipe with ¼ teaspoon cinnamon, in place of oregano, for a totally different flavor.

## Nutrition Facts

Per serving:  Calories 72 (30% calories from fat)  Fat 2.6 g (saturated fat .3 g)
Protein 2 g  Carbohydrates 9.5 g  Fiber 1.5 g  Cholesterol 0  Sodium 302 mg.

# SUMMER VEGETABLES GRILLED WITH HERB DRESSING

| | |
|---|---|
| 2 | garlic cloves, crushed |
| 2 | tablespoons olive oil |
| 1 | red bell pepper, cored, seeded and cut into quarters |
| 1 | yellow bell pepper, cored, seeded cut into quarters |
| 2 | small zucchini, cut lengthwise |
| 2 | large portobello mushroom, quartered |
| 4 | green onion, trimmed |
| 4 | small new potatoes, cooked and halved |
| | Salt & pepper to taste |

## Herb Dressing:

| | |
|---|---|
| 1 | teaspoon minced fresh savory or tarragon |
| ½ | teaspoon crushed, dried thyme |
| ¼ | teaspoon freshly ground black pepper |
| | Salt to taste |
| 2 | tablespoons balsamic vinegar |

Combine garlic and olive oil in a cup and set aside for 30 minutes. Brush peppers, zucchini, mushrooms, green onions and potatoes with garlic oil. Place vegetables in a grilling basket and grill over medium-high heat for about 15 minutes or until done. (Some vegetables may cook quicker than others depending on their thickness; remove these first.)

While vegetables are grilling prepare herb dressing as follows. Combine savory, thyme, pepper, salt and balsamic vinegar. Stir well to blend. Place cooked vegetables in a bowl. Pour herb dressing over the top and toss gently. Adjust seasonings and serve at room temperature. Yield: 4 servings.

## Nutrition Facts

Per serving: Calories 148 (40% calories from fat) Fat 7 g (saturated fat 1 g Protein 4.5 g Carbohydrates 20 g Fiber 5.5 g Cholesterol 0 Sodium 16 mg.

# WASHINGTON STATE KALE-STUFFED TOMATOES

| | |
|---|---|
| 8 | red ripe medium-sized tomatoes |
| ¾ | pound fresh kale, stems discarded and leaves rinsed well |
| 2 | tablespoons olive oil |
| 1 | medium onion, chopped |
| 3 | garlic cloves, minced |
| ⅛ | teaspoon red pepper flakes |
| 1 ¼ | cup water, divided |
| | Salt and pepper to taste |
| 1 | tablespoon cornstarch |
| ⅔ | cup chicken broth |
| 3 | tablespoons Parmesan cheese |

Cut top off of each tomato and scoop out the pulp two thirds down to the bottom. Discard seeds and chop the fleshy part and place it in a mixing bowl. Place tomatoes on a foil-lined baking pan. Shred the kale and place in the mixing bowl with the tomato pulp.

Heat a large skillet over medium heat, add the olive oil and sauté the chopped onion and garlic until onion is softened. Add the kale and tomato, ½ cup of water, salt and pepper to taste; cook the mixture, covered, stirring occasionally and adding the remaining water gradually over a 15-minute period. The kale should be tender. If there is excess liquid, boil uncovered, until the liquid is absorbed. Stir the cornstarch into the chicken broth and add to the kale. Simmer, stirring, for 1 minute, or until it is thickened. Remove the skillet from the heat, stir in the Parmesan and fill the tomatoes. Bake in a pre-heated 350° oven for 12-15 minutes, or until tomatoes are cooked, but firm. Yield: 8 servings.

## Nutrition Facts

Per serving:  Calories 92 (42% calories from fat)  Fat 4.7 g (saturated fat 1 g) Protein 4 g Carbohydrates 11 g Fiber 2.5 g Cholesterol 2 mg Sodium 38 mg.

# WEST PALM BEACH ROASTED GARLIC

3    whole garlic bulbs
1    teaspoon olive oil

Peel away the dry outer leaves of each garlic bulb. Slice about ¼-inch off the top, exposing each individual clove. Place the garlic bulbs in a small, covered baking dish, cut side up. Drizzle or brush olive oil over the tops of the garlic cloves and cover with aluminum foil. (A clay garlic baker may be used, if available).

Bake the garlic in a pre-heated 350° oven for 45 minutes or until the garlic is soft. The garlic paste should press easily from each clove and can be spread on crusty bread. Yield: 12 servings.

## Nutrition Facts

Per serving: Calories 16 (22% calories from fat) Fat .4 g (saturated fat 0) Protein .5 g Carbohydrates 3 g Fiber .2 g Cholesterol 0 Sodium 2 mg.

# WILMINGTON'S VEGETABLE POTSTICKERS

1 ½ cups fat-free chicken broth
1 medium onion, finely chopped
1 stalk celery, finely chopped
½ cup finely chopped mushroom
½ cup finely chopped cabbage
2 garlic cloves, minced
1 teaspoon grated gingerroot
1 teaspoon soy sauce
1 teaspoon sesame oil
30 won-ton wrappers (½ of a 16-ounce package)
Sweet and sour sauce or additional soy sauce for serving (optional)

Heat a non-stick skillet over medium-high heat. Add ½ cup of the chicken broth and bring to a simmer. Add the onion, celery, mushrooms, cabbage, garlic and gingerroot. Cook about 10 minutes, or until vegetables are tender and liquid is absorbed. (You may add additional chicken broth if needed.) Remove vegetables from skillet, place in a bowl and stir in the soy sauce and sesame oil. Set aside. Wash and dry skillet.

Assemble the potstickers as follows: working with 4 or 5 wrappers at a time, spread them out on a work surface. Using a pastry brush, moisten two edges of each wrapper. Place about ¾ teaspoon of vegetables in the center and fold wrapper over into a triangle shape. Press edges together to seal and crimp corners together to form a won ton. You will quickly get the feel of how much stuffing should be used after 2 or 3 are done. Assemble all of the potstickers and place them in single layer.

Return the non-stick skillet to medium-high heat. Spray the skillet with vegetable cooking spray. Cook the filled won tons by batches, until the bottoms brown. You may turn them and brown on another side if you wish, spraying the pan with each new batch. Add remaining broth to another saucepan and simmer the cooked won tons 3 to 5 minutes until they are tender. Remove one batch at a time, and serve warm with soy sauce and sweet and sour sauce if desired. Yield: 10 servings.

## Nutrition Facts

Per serving: Calories 90 (9% calories from fat) Fat 1 g (saturated fat .1 g) Protein 4 g Carbohydrates 16.5 g Fiber 1 g Cholesterol 2 mg Sodium 186 mg.

# Pasta & Grains

# Pasta & Grains

# BIG SUR SPAGHETTI IN SAND

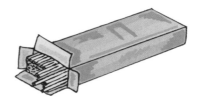

| | |
|---|---|
| 12 | ounces spaghetti, uncooked |
| 3 | tablespoons olive oil |
| 2 | cloves garlic, minced |
| 1 | dried (or 1 teaspoon fresh) chile pepper, chopped |
| ¼ | cup Italian-style breadcrumbs |
| 2 | tablespoons fresh chopped parsley |
| ⅓ | cup white wine, or chicken broth |
| ¼ | cup fat-free Parmesan cheese |

Fill a large saucepan with salted water and bring to a boil. Cook spaghetti to the 'al dente' stage. In a separate skillet, heat the olive oil over medium heat. Add garlic and chile pepper; sauté for 2 minutes. Add the breadcrumbs, toss and cook 2 minutes more. Stir in wine and parsley; heat through and toss with cooked pasta. Season with salt and pepper if desired, sprinkle with Parmesan cheese and serve immediately. Yield: 4 servings.

## Nutrition Facts

Per serving:  Calories 445 (24% calories from fat)  Fat 12 g (saturated fat 1.5 g)
Protein 14 g Carbohydrates 70 g Fiber 2.5 g Cholesterol 1.4 mg Socium 213 mg.

# COCOA BEACH CREAMY PEAS & PASTA

| | |
|---|---|
| 1 | cup fresh shelled peas (uncooked frozen may be used) |
| 1 | tablespoon butter |
| 1 | garlic clove, minced |
| ¼ | cup dry sherry |
| ¾ | cup non-fat half & half |
| ¾ | cup fat-free Parmesan cheese |
| 2 | ounces lean ham, cut into thin strips |
| 4 | ounces linguini, cooked according to directions |
| ¼ | teaspoon black pepper |

Partially cook fresh peas in boiling water to cover about 5 minutes or until they are crisp, then drain. (Do not cook frozen peas.) Heat a non-stick skillet over medium heat and add the butter to melt. Add garlic and sauté 2 minutes or until tender. Stir in sherry and cook until reduced by half (about 5 minutes). Reduce heat to medium; stir in half & half and bring to a simmer. Whisk in cheese until smooth. Stir in cooked linguini, peas, ham and pepper. Serve immediately. Yield: 2 servings.

NOTE: This recipe is good to use with fresh or frozen lima beans as well.

## Nutrition Facts

Per serving: Calories 495 (16% calories from fat) Fat 8.5 g (saturated fat 2.8 g) Protein 34 g Carbohydrates 65 g Fiber 6.5 g Cholesterol 25 mg Sodium 1027 mg.

*For days on the run with no time to cook, try the veggie-salad bar for quick salad-suppers, vegetable stir-frys or easy pasta dishes.*

# FETTUCCINE WITH SEA BASS & OLIVE SAUCE

|       |                                      |
|-------|--------------------------------------|
| 2     | tablespoons butter                   |
| 4     | shallots, chopped                    |
| 2     | tablespoons capers                   |
| 1     | cup pimento-stuffed olives, chopped  |
| 4     | tablespoons balsamic vinegar         |
| 1 ¼   | cups fish stock or chicken broth     |
| 1 ¼   | cups fat-free half and half          |
| 1     | tablespoon fresh lemon juice         |
|       | Salt and pepper to taste             |
| 2     | pounds sea bass medallions           |
| 1     | tablespoon canola oil                |
| 1     | pound of fettuccine cooked al dente  |
|       | Sliced leek for garnish              |

Place skillet over medium heat and melt the butter. Add the shallots and cook for 3 or 4 minutes. Add the capers and olives and cook 3 minutes more. Stir in the balsamic vinegar and fish stock, bring to a boil and simmer until liquid is reduced by half. Add the cream, stirring and reduce again by half. Stir in the lemon juice, season to taste with salt and pepper and set the pan aside.

Brush sea bass medallions lightly with oil. Broil 3-4 minutes on each side until they are cooked, but still moist. Divide cooked pasta equally onto six serving plates, place medallions on top and ladle sauce over all. Garnish with sliced leek. Yield: 6 servings.

## Nutrition Facts

Per serving:  Calories 552 (28% calories from fat)  Fat 17 g (saturated fat 2.7 g)
Protein 42 g  Carbohydrates 54 g  Fiber 3 g  Cholesterol 124 mg  Sodium 1060 mg.

*Fat-free chicken broth can be used in place of oil or butter in sautéed dishes, saving 14 grams of fat for every tablespoon it replaces.*

# KEY WEST YELLOW-RICE WITH BLACK BEANS & CORN

| | |
|---|---|
| 1 | teaspoon olive oil |
| 1 | cup diced onion |
| 2 | cloves garlic, crushed |
| 1 | cup long-grain rice, uncooked |
| 2 | cups water |
| ¼ | teaspoon saffron threads |
| ½ | cup canned black beans, drained |
| ¼ | cup whole kernel corn |
| | Salt and pepper to taste |

Spray a large non-stick skillet with vegetable cooking spray. Place over medium-high heat, add oil and heat until hot. Add onion and garlic, sauté for 2 minutes. Add rice and sauté 2 minutes more. Add water and saffron. Cover, reduce heat and simmer 20-25 minutes or until liquid is absorbed and rice is tender. Stir in black beans and corn; cook 5 minutes or until thoroughly heated. Add salt and pepper, if desired. Yield: 4 servings.

## Nutrition Facts

Per serving:  Calories 170 (9% calories from fat)  Fat 1.6 g (saturated fat .2 g)
Protein 5 g  Carbohydrates 33 g  Fiber 3 g  Cholesterol 0  Sodium 45 mg.

*Pasta & Grains*

# LASAGNA WITH EGGPLANT & SPINACH

| | |
|---|---|
| 1 | medium-size, purple eggplant |
| | Salt for soaking |
| 2 | tablespoons olive oil |
| ½ | cup chopped onion |
| 2 | cloves minced garlic |
| 1 | (28-ounce) can Italian crushed tomatoes |
| 1 | tablespoon sugar |
| 2 | teaspoons Italian seasoning |
| | Salt & pepper to taste |
| 1 | egg |
| 1 | tablespoon 1% milk |
| ⅔ | cup seasoned bread crumbs |
| 1 | (8-ounce) box no-cook lasagna noodles |
| 1 | cup 1% fat cottage cheese |
| 1 ½ | cups tender spinach leaves, washed and drained |
| ½ | cup fat-free Parmesan cheese, divided |
| 4 | ounces part-skim Mozzarella cheese, shredded |
| 3 | tablespoons chopped parsley |

Slice eggplant into ¼-inch rounds. Layer eggplant in a colander over the sink and sprinkle with salt and water. Allow eggplant to sit for 20-30 minutes to drain out any bitter flavor.

At the same time, begin the sauce by heating the olive oil in a 2-quart saucepan over medium heat. Add the chopped onion and sauté for 2 minutes until the onion is soft. Add the garlic and sauté one minute more. Carefully stir in the tomatoes so they do not spatter. Add sugar, Italian seasoning, salt and pepper if desired. Simmer for 30 minutes, stirring occasionally until tomatoes soften and the sauce thickens.

While the tomatoes cook, prepare the eggplant slices. Remove them from the colander and pat with paper towels to absorb any water. Lightly beat 1 egg with milk in a small bowl. Place breadcrumbs in a second bowl. Dip each eggplant slice into egg mixture on one side, then place that side down into the breadcrumbs, coating one side only. Cook eggplant slices in a non-stick skillet sprayed with vegetable cooking spray, coated side first. Turn when browned and cook on second side for a minute or two. You may need to spray the pan after each batch of eggplant.

(Note that the eggplant slices do not need to be thoroughly cooked). When all eggplant is browned, salt it, set it aside and prepare the cottage cheese. Place the cottage cheese and the second egg in a blender and process until mixture is smooth. You are now ready to assemble the dish.

Use a baking pan that is 11"x7"x2" high. Spread a layer of sauce over the bottom of the pan and cover it with lasagna noodles. Layer the eggplant next, top with fresh spinach leaves, then spoon more sauce over that.

Using about ⅓ of the cottage cheese mixture, place teaspoons full over that layer. Sprinkle with Mozzarella and Parmesan. Complete two more layers as just assembled, using all of your ingredients as equally as you can. (Save some tomato sauce for spooning at the table). Bake lasagna in a preheated 350° oven for 45-55 minutes until it is bubbly and brown on top. Sprinkle with parsley, season of desired and serve. Yield: 6 servings.

### Nutrition Facts

Per serving: Calories 366 (27% calories from fat)  Fat 11 g (saturated fat 4 g)
Protein 27 g  Carbohydrates 40 g  Fiber 6 g  Cholesterol 49 mg  Sodium 1095 mg.

# LOUISIANA RED BEANS & RICE

| | |
|---|---|
| 1 | tablespoon canola oil |
| 2 | medium onion, chopped |
| 2 | garlic cloves, minced |
| 2 | cups diced pumpkin or squash |
| 2 | teaspoon curry powder |
| 1 | teaspoon salt |
| ½ | teaspoon black pepper |
| ¼ | teaspoon ground cloves |
| 3 | cups water |
| 1 ½ | cups long grain white rice |
| 1 | cup chopped fresh kale |
| 1 | (15-ounce) can red kidney beans |

In a large saucepan, heat the oil over medium heat. Add the onion and saute for 2 minutes; add the garlic and saute 1 or 2 minutes more, until both vegetables are soft. Stir in the pumpkin, curry powder, salt, pepper and cloves; cook for 1 minute. Add water and rice, cover and cook for 15 minutes on low heat. Stir in kale and beans and cook for 5 minutes more. Turn off heat and fluff rice. Let stand for 10 minutes before serving. Yield: 6 servings.

### Nutrition Facts

Per serving: Calories 306 (9% calories from fat)  Fat 3 g (saturated fat .3 g)  Protein 10 g  Carbohydrates 60 g  Fiber 8 g  Cholesterol 0  Sodium 203 mg.

# MEDITERRANEAN LENTILS & COUSCOUS

| | |
|---|---|
| 1 | (14 ½-ounce) can low-sodium chicken broth |
| 1 | (14 ½-ounce) can diced tomatoes |
| 1 | teaspoon salt |
| ½ | teaspoon crushed red pepper |
| ½ | teaspoon dried basil |
| ½ | teaspoon oregano |
| 10 | ounces quick-cooking couscous |
| 1 ½ | cups cooked lentils |
| 2 | tablespoons olive oil |
| 4 | diced green onions |
| ½ | cup diced green bell pepper |
| ¼ | cup chopped fresh parsley |
| 1 | diced celery rib |
| 2 | cloves garlic, minced |

Stir together the chicken broth, undrained tomatoes, salt, red pepper, basil and oregano in a large saucepan, over medium-high heat and bring to a boil. Remove from heat and stir in the couscous; let stand for 10 minutes. Fluff mixture with a fork and stir in drained and cooked lentils. Set mixture aside.

Heat olive oil in a non-stick skillet. Add onions, bell pepper, celery and garlic. Sauté for about 2 minutes. Remove from heat and add couscous mixture, tossing to blend all . Turn out into a serving dish and sprinkle with parsley. Yield: 8 servings.

## Nutrition Facts

Per serving:  Calories 227 (17% calories from fat)  Fat 4 g (saturated fat .7 g) Protein 9 g  Carbohydrates 38 g  Fiber 4 g  Cholesterol 1 mg  Sodium 355 mg.

*Toss cooked pasta with tomato-based sauces or stir-fried vegetables. The result will be healthier than using high-fat creamy sauces.*

# PACIFIC COAST CRAB CANNELLONI

| | |
|---|---|
| 8 | fresh or no-cook lasagna sheets (5x6 ½") |
| 1 ½ | cups part-skim ricotta cheese |
| 1 | egg, lightly beaten |
| 1 | teaspoon fresh parsley, chopped |
| 1 | teaspoon snipped chive |
| ⅛ | teaspoon salt |
| ⅛ | teaspoon white pepper |
| | Dash nutmeg |
| 8 | ounces steamed crab meat (any variety) |

Prepare lasagna sheets for handling by blanching until softened; set aside.

In a medium mixing bowl, place ricotta cheese, beaten egg, parsley, chive and seasonings. Blend with a wooden spoon. Gently stir in crab meat, trying not to break up crab meat lumps.

To assemble cannelloni, place filling equally down center of each pasta sheet. Roll up tightly to form a thick tube. Spray a baking dish with non-fat cooking spray and arrange cannelloni in the dish. You may cover and refrigerate at this point to be cooked within 48 hours.

To bake cannelloni, pre-heat oven to 350°. Spoon your favorite pasta sauce over tubes and bake for 20 minutes, or until heated through. Serve immediately. Yield: 8 servings.

NOTE: This dish is delicious with the Marinara sauce recipe for rigatoni in this chapter.

## Nutrition Facts

Per serving:  Calories 203 (24% calories from fat)  Fat 5 g (saturated fat 2.5 g)
Protein 15.5 g Carbohydrates 23 g Fiber 1 g Cholesterol 69 mg Sodium 146 mg.

# PANAMA CITY PASTA WITH ROASTED VEGETABLES

| | |
|---|---|
| 1 | yellow bell pepper, chopped |
| 1 | medium-size red onion, sliced |
| 1 | medium zucchini, chopped |
| 2 | tablespoons olive oil |
| ½ | teaspoon salt |
| ¼ | teaspoon black pepper |
| 2 | large tomatoes, chopped |
| 3 | tablespoons fresh basil, chopped |
| 2 | cloves garlic, minced |
| | Additional salt and pepper to taste |
| 12 | ounces favorite pasta or spaghetti, uncooked |
| ½ | cup feta cheese, crumbled |

In a large mixing bowl, toss the bell pepper, onion and zucchini together with 1 tablespoon olive oil, salt and pepper. Spray a large roasting pan with cooking spray. Roast vegetables in a pre-heated 450° oven for 15 to 20 minutes, stirring occasionally, until they are tender and browned.

At the same time, heat a large saucepan of water to boil the pasta. Meanwhile, combine tomatoes, basil, garlic and remaining 1 tablespoon of olive oil. Season to taste with salt and pepper. Cook pasta to the "firm" stage, about 8-10 minutes. Remove from heat, drain and place in a large serving bowl, with the tomatoes. Stir in the roasted vegetables and toss well. Sprinkle the feta cheese on top and serve immediately. Yield: 4 servings.

## Nutrition Facts

Per serving: Calories 473 (24% calories from fat) Fat 12 g (saturated fat 4 g) Protein 15.5 g Carbohydrates 75 g Fiber 5 g Cholesterol 17 mg Sodium 516 mg.

*Pasta & Grains*

# PASTA PRIMAVERA WITH ALFREDO SAUCE

| | |
|---|---|
| 3 | tablespoons 1% milk |
| 1 ½ | cups lowfat cottage cheese |
| ½ | cup sweet red bell pepper, chopped |
| 1 | cup sliced fresh mushrooms |
| 1 | fresh garlic clove, minced |
| 1 | tablespoon light margarine |
| ½ | cup frozen green peas |
| ¼ | teaspoon each salt & pepper |
| 8 | ounces dry fettuccine noodles |
| 2 | tablespoons Parmesan cheese |
| 1 | tablespoon fresh basil, chopped |

Combine milk and cottage cheese in a blender and blend until smooth. In a medium saucepan, cook the sweet pepper, mushrooms and garlic in margarine until tender. Reduce heat; add cheese mixture, peas, salt and pepper. Cook on low, stirring, until heated through, making sure mixture does not boil. Remove from heat and set aside.

Cook fettuccine noodles according to package directions. Toss cooked fettuccine with cheese mixture. Sprinkle with Parmesan cheese and basil and serve. Yield: 4 servings.

## Nutrition Facts

Per serving:  Calories 268 (16% calories from fat)  Fat 5 g (saturated fat 1.7 g)
Protein 19 g  Carbohydrates 39 g  Fiber 3 g  Cholesterol 15 mg  Sodium 650 mg.

# RIGATONI WITH MARINARA SAUCE

| | |
|---|---|
| 1 | small onion, chopped |
| 2 | garlic cloves, minced |
| 2 | tablespoons olive oil |
| 2 | (28-ounce) cans Italian peeled tomatoes |
| | Salt and pepper to taste |
| 2 | teaspoons sugar |
| ¼ | cup dry white wine |
| ½ | cup fresh parsley, chopped |
| 2 | tablespoons fresh basil, chopped |
| 16 | ounces rigatoni pasta, dry |

Heat a large saucepan over medium-hot heat. Sauté onion and garlic in olive oil, until transparent (about 2 minutes). Add tomatoes, salt and pepper to taste and sugar. Bring to a boil, add white wine, parsley and basil.

Reduce heat to medium-low and simmer about 30 minutes or until tomatoes have softened and cooked down. Adjust seasoning, remove from heat and set aside while pasta cooks.

Cook rigatoni according to package directions. Drain well and serve sauce over rigatoni immediately. Yield: 6 servings.

## Nutrition Facts

Per serving: Calories 381 (17% calories from fat) Fat 6.6 g (saturated fat 1.4 g)
Protein 15.5 g Carbohydrates 84 g Fiber 7.4 g Cholesterol 0 Sodium 398 mg.

# RISOTTO WITH SPINACH & MUSHROOMS

| | |
|---|---|
| 2 | tablespoons olive oil |
| 1 | medium onion, chopped |
| 2 | cups arborio rice |
| 1 | cup fresh mushrooms, chopped |
| ½ | cup dry white wine |
| | Salt and pepper to taste |
| ⅛ | teaspoon saffron, softened in 1 tablespoon hot water |
| 5 | cups fat-free chicken broth |
| 1 | cup fresh spinach, chopped |
| 2 | tablespoons butter |
| ¼ | cup grated fat-free Parmesan cheese |

Heat olive oil in a large skillet with a tight-fitting lid. Add chopped onion and sauté about 3 minutes until soft. Add rice, mushrooms and wine, stirring as you add. Season with salt and pepper to taste, add saffron and 1 cup of the chicken broth. Reduce heat and simmer rice covered, until the liquid has been absorbed. Add spinach and more chicken broth, continuing to add broth one cup at a time, until all the chicken broth has been used and the rice is tender. (You may add more chicken broth or water, if necessary). This rice will cook in about 30 minutes. To serve, add butter, stir to melt and mix in Parmesan Cheese. Yield: 8 servings.

## Nutrition Facts

Per serving: Calories 286 (21% calories from fat) Fat 6.5 g (saturated 1.5 g) Protein 10 g  Carbohydrates 43 g  Fiber 2 g  Cholesterol 4 mg  Sodium 246 mg.

*When preparing packaged mixes of pasta, rice or stuffing, use only half the butter  or oil called  for in the directions.  You will cut the fat, but not the flavor.*

# ROASTED BELL PEPPERS & PENNE PASTA

| | |
|---|---|
| 1 | yellow bell pepper, sliced |
| 1 | red bell pepper, sliced |
| 1 | green bell pepper, sliced |
| 1 | large onion, thinly sliced |
| 4 | teaspoons olive oil |
| | Salt and pepper to taste |
| 2 | large tomatoes, chopped |
| ¼ | cup chopped fresh basil |
| 2 | cloves garlic, minced |
| 12 | ounces penne pasta |
| ¼ | cup fat-free Parmesan cheese |

Pre-heat oven to 450°. In a large mixing bowl, toss peppers and onions with 2 teaspoons olive oil. Place in a large roasting pan and season with salt and pepper. Roast vegetables, stirring occasionally until they are tender and brown. This should take about 15 minutes. In a separate bowl, combine tomatoes, basil, garlic and remaining 2 teaspoons of oil. Season with salt and pepper.

Cook pasta according to package directions. Drain and toss with tomato mixture. Add roast vegetables, adjust seasoning and sprinkle with Parmesan. Toss gently to blend . Serve immediately. Yield: 4 servings.

## Nutrition Facts

Per serving: Calories 340 (17% calories from fat) Fat 6.7 g (saturated fat .7 g Protein 13 g Carbohydrates 61 g Fiber 5.5 g Cholesterol 1 mg Sodium 258 mg.

# ROTINI PASTA HUNTER'S-STYLE

2    ounces dried mushrooms (any blend)
3    tablespoons olive oil
1    medium-size onion, chopped
1    celery stalk, sliced
1    garlic clove, minced
4    slices Canadian bacon, chopped
⅓    cup white wine
2    ounces smoked turkey sausage, chopped
½    cup frozen peas, defrosted
1    bay leaf
½    cup fat-free half & half
1    (16-ounce) box Fusilli pasta
¼    cup fat-free Parmesan cheese
    Salt & pepper to taste

Soak mushrooms in warm water to re-hydrate; set aside. Heat oil in a saucepan and sauté onion, celery and garlic until browned. Add bacon and wine and bay leaf; bring to a slow simmer and cook until the wine evaporates. Add peas, mushrooms (discarding liquid), sausage and half & half. Simmer on low for 15 minutes.

While this is cooking, start the pasta in a large pot of salted water and cook until it has reached the 'al dente' stage. Remove from heat, drain and put pasta in a large serving bowl. Remove the bay leaf from the sauce and pour over the pasta. Sprinkle with Parmesan cheese and seasoning if desired and serve. Yield: 6 servings.

## Nutrition Facts

Per serving:  Calories 295 (30% calories from fat)  Fat 9.6 g)  saturated fat 1.7 g)
Protein 15 g  Carbohydrates 33 g  Fiber 5 g  Cholesterol 16 mg  Sodium 435 mg.

## SHELL PASTA WITH WHITE CLAM SAUCE

| | |
|---|---|
| 10 | ounces dried pasta shells (for 4 servings) |
| 2 | tablespoons olive oil |
| 1 | medium onion, chopped |
| 3 | cloves fresh garlic, minced |
| 2 | teaspoons lemon juice |
| ½ | cup white wine |
| 1 | tablespoon fresh basil, chopped |
| 2 | teaspoons dried thyme |
| ½ | teaspoon crushed red pepper |
| 2 | (6 ½-ounce) cans chopped clams with juice |
| ¼ | cup chopped fresh parsley |
| ½ | cup fat-free Parmesan cheese |

Prepare pasta according to package directions. While pasta is cooking, heat olive oil in a sauté pan and sauté the onion and garlic, until onion is clear. Add lemon juice, wine, basil, thyme and red pepper. Heat slowly to the simmer point. Remove from heat and add clams. Drain pasta when cooked, add to clam sauce and allow the pasta to absorb the juices for a few minutes. Toss and serve on individual plates. Garnish with parsley and Parmesan. Serve immediately. Yield: 4 servings.

### Nutrition Facts

Per serving: Calories 377 (20% calories from fat) Fat 8.5 g (saturated 1.3 g) Protein 15 g  Carbohydrates 57 g  Fiber 3.5 g  Cholesterol 5 mg  Sodium 400 mg.


## SOUTHERN PECAN RICE

| | |
|---|---|
| 1 | cup long-grain white rice |
| 2 | cups fat-free chicken broth |
| ½ | cup chopped onions |
| ¾ | ounce pecans, chopped fine |
| 1 | cup frozen peas, thawed |
| 1 | tablespoon lightly salted butter or margarine |

Combine rice, chicken broth and onions in a medium saucepan and bring to a boil. Reduce the heat and simmer 20 minutes, or until the rice is cooked. Fold in pecans and peas. Season with salt, pepper and butter. Serve immediately. Yield: 6 servings.

### Nutrition Facts

Per serving:  Calories 188 (22% calories from fat)  Fat 4.5 g (saturated fat 1.5 g Protein 6 g  Carbohydrates 30 g  Fiber 2.4 g  Cholesterol 5 mg  Sodium 101 mg.

# TAGLIATELLE WITH CARAMELIZED ONIONS AND GREENS

| | |
|---|---|
| 1 | tablespoon olive oil |
| 1 | tablespoon unsalted butter |
| 4 | medium onions, peeled and cut into thick rings |
| 1 | teaspoon sugar |
| ½ | cup white wine |
| 3 ½ | cups fat-free chicken broth |
| | Salt and pepper to taste |
| 1 | pound tagliatelle (or fettuccine) pasta |
| 1 | head mustard greens, broccoli rabe or kale, washed, trimmed, torn into pieces, and cooked |

Heat a large, heavy skillet (preferably not non-stick) over medium-high heat. Add oil, butter and heat. Add onions and sugar and cook, stirring occasionally, until well browned, about 10 minutes. Turn heat to low; continue to cook, until very soft, about another 10 minutes.

Remove half the onions and set aside. Add wine to de-glaze, scraping the bottom of the pan. Add chicken broth and bring to a boil. Cook over high heat for 10 minutes, season to taste with salt and pepper.

Cook pasta to the "al dente" stage, or just under the time called for on the package. (Pasta must be firm). Drain and add to broth; bring to a slow simmer. Add cooked greens and simmer, covered about 2 minutes, or until warmed through. Place in a serving bowl with reserved onions on top. Serve while hot. Yield: 6 servings.

## Nutrition Facts

Per serving: Calories 307 (17% calories from fat) Fat 6 g (saturated fat 1 g) Protein 12 g  Carbohydrates 49 g  Fiber 4 g  Cholesterol 2 mg  Sodium 262 mg.

*Why is water good for you?  It has no calories or fat, fills you up when you drink it with meals and allows the body to carry out all of it's functions.  So drink up—8 glasses a day.*

# TORTELLINI WITH CHICKEN & HERB SAUCE

| | |
|---|---|
| 2 | tablespoons olive oil |
| 1 | red onion, cut into wedges |
| 12 | ounces cheese-filled tortellini |
| 1 | garlic clove, chopped |
| 2 ½ | cups boned chicken breast, diced |
| 1 ¼ | cups dry white wine |
| 3 | tablespoons chopped fresh herbs (or 1 teaspoon Italian seasoning) |
| ⅔ | cup part-skim ricotta cheese |
| | Salt and pepper to taste |
| | Parsley sprigs for garnish |

Heat a large non-stick frying pan and spray with vegetable cooking spray. Add 1 tablespoon olive oil and when it is hot, add the onion. Sauté onion for 10 minutes, or until softened and the layers separate. During this time, start cooking the tortellini, following the package directions.

When onion is ready, add the second tablespoon of olive oil to the pan and allow to heat. Stir in the garlic and the chicken; cook, stirring occasionally, until the chicken is browned and cooked through. Pour in the wine, bring to a boil and cook until reduced by half. Stir in the herbs, ricotta and heat through, stirring gently and being careful not to boil. Season with salt and pepper to taste, and toss with cooked tortellini to coat. Garnish with fresh parsley and serve. Yield: 6 servings.

## Nutrition Facts

Per serving:  Calories 310 (32% calories from fat)  Fat 11 g (saturated fat 3.5 g)
Protein 23.5 g  Carbohydrates 21 g  Fiber 2 g  Cholesterol 57 mg  Sodium 249 mg.

# VIRGINIAL HAM, CHEESE & BROCCOLI GRITS

| | |
|---|---|
| 1 | quart 1% milk |
| ½ | teaspoon salt |
| 1 | cup uncooked quick grits |
| 6 | ounces extra-lean ham, chopped |
| 16 | ounces frozen broccoli pieces, thawed and pressed dry |
| 4 | ounces low-fat Cheddar cheese, shredded |
| 1 | small onion, shredded |
| 1 | large egg |

Pour milk and salt into a 3-quart saucepan and slowly bring to a gentle boil over medium heat. Whisk in grits and reduce heat to a simmer. Cook stirring often, 7 to 8 minutes until thickened. Stir in ham, broccoli and all but 2 tablespoons of cheese. Add onion and egg and stir just until blended. Pour into a shallow 2-quart baking dish that has been sprayed with vegetable cooking spray.

Bake in a pre-heated 375° oven for 15 minutes. Sprinkle with reserved cheese and bake 10 to 15 minutes more until bubbly. Yield: 6 servings.

## Nutrition Facts

Per serving: Calories 282 (19% calories from fat) Fat 6 g (saturated 2.7 g) Protein 22 g Carbohydrates 35 g Fiber 3 g Cholesterol 67 mg Sodium 762 mg.

# Meat & Poultry

# Meat & Poultry

# ASIAN BEEF AND GREEN BEANS OVER RICE

| | |
|---|---|
| 1 | pound fresh green beans |
| 1 | tablespoon cornstarch |
| ½ | teaspoon ground ginger |
| 2 | tablespoons soy sauce |
| 6 | garlic cloves, minced |
| 12 | ounces boneless top round, sirloin or flank steak |
| 1 | tablespoon peanut oil (divided into 3 teaspoons) |
| 2 | tablespoons smooth peanut butter |
| 1 | tablespoon lime juice |
| 2 | tablespoons chopped fresh cilantro |
| 4 | cups hot cooked rice |

Wash, trim and cut beans into 2-inch lengths. Blanch beans for 3 minutes in boiling water to tenderize them before stir-frying.

In a medium bowl, mix cornstarch, ginger, 1 teaspoon of soy sauce and half the garlic. Cut beef into thin strips and marinate in the soy sauce mixture. Heat 1 tablespoon of oil in a large non-stick skillet over medium heat. Add beans and stir-fry for 3 minutes, or until beans are slightly scorched. Add remaining garlic and stir-fry 1 minute more. Transfer beans to a bowl.

Mix peanut butter in 1 cup of hot water; add the remaining 1 tablespoon soy sauce and set aside. In the same skillet, heat the remaining 2 teaspoons of the oil over medium-high heat. Add beef, a little at a time, stirring constantly. Stir-fry 3 minutes or until beef is browned. Stir in beans and peanut butter mixture. Cook, stirring often, 1 minute or until mixture is heated through and sauce is slightly thickened. Stir in lime juice. Remove from heat and sprinkle with cilantro. Serve over rice. Yield: 4 servings.

## Nutrition Facts

Per serving: Calories 539 (32% calories from fat) Fat 19 g (saturated fat 6 g) Protein 25 g Carbohydrates 66 g Fiber 2.4 g Cholesterol 55 mg Sodium 270 mg.

# BRUNSWICK BOURBON CHICKEN KABOBS

| | |
|---|---|
| 6 | 4-ounce boneless chicken breast halves, skinned |
| ¼ | cup teriyaki sauce |
| 1 | tablespoon gingerroot, peeled and grated |
| 3 | tablespoons bourbon |
| 2 | tablespoons honey |
| 2 | teaspoons sesame oil |
| 2 | cloves garlic, minced |
| 6 | green onions, cut into 1-inch pieces |
| 18 | cherry tomatoes |
| ⅔ | cup pineapple chunks |
| 2 | small green bell peppers (or 1 large) cut in 12 pieces |
| | Vegetable cooking spray |

Cut each chicken breast half into 4 or 5 bite-sized chunks. Combine teriyaki sauce, gingerroot, bourbon, honey, sesame oil and garlic in a heavy-duty, zip-top plastic bag. Add chicken and green onion; seal bag, and shake until well coated. Marinate in refrigerator 3 hours, turning bag occasionally.

Allow 30 minutes before cooking preparation, to soak 6 bamboo skewers in water. Remove chicken and green onions from marinade; discard marinade. Thread chicken and green onions alternately with whole cherry tomatoes and green pepper pieces equally between 6 skewers. Coat grill rack with vegetable cooking spray; place on grill over medium-hot coals (350-400°). Place skewers on rack; grill, covered, 2-3 minutes on each side or until done. Yield: 6 servings.

NOTE: This dish goes well served over KEY WEST YELLOW-RICE WITH BLACK BEANS & CORN.

## Nutrition Facts

Per serving: Calories 255 (29% calories from fat)  Fat 8 g (saturated fat 2 g)  Protein 25 g  Carbohydrates 15 g  Fiber 1.8 g  Cholesterol 68 mg  Sodium 238 mg.

# BURGUNDY & MUSTARD MARINATED SIRLOIN

| | |
|---|---|
| 2 | tablespoons Dijon mustard |
| 2 | tablespoons Burgundy wine |
| 1 | teaspoon coarsely ground pepper |
| 2 | cloves garlic, minced |
| 1 | pound lean, boneless sirloin steak, trimmed |
| 1 | cup fresh, sliced mushrooms |
| 1 ½ | tablespoons all-purpose flour |
| 1 | cup fat-free beef broth |
| ½ | cup Burgundy wine |
| ¼ | teaspoon salt |
| ¼ | teaspoon black pepper |

Combine Dijon mustard, Burgundy, ground pepper and garlic. Coat steak on both sides with mustard mixture, and place in a shallow dish. Cover and refrigerate for at least 4 hours.

Broil or grill steak as desired over or under medium-high heat, until just under desired degree of doneness. Let stand 5 minutes. Slice steak thinly, across grain and keep warm.

Coat a non-stick skillet with cooking spray; add mushrooms and cook, stirring constantly, over medium heat until tender. Add flour and cook 1 minute, stirring constantly. Gradually add beef broth and ½ cup of Burgundy, stirring constantly until thickened. Stir in salt and pepper and pour over meat. Serve immediately. Yield: 4 servings.

## Nutrition Facts

Per serving:  Calories 232 (30% calories from fat)  Fat 7.7 g (saturated fat 2.7 g)
Protein 29 g  Carbohydrates 5 g  Fiber .5 g  Cholesterol 77 mg  Sodium 412 mg.

*Baking, broiling, roasting and grilling meats will allow fat to drip away.*

# CAPE MAY CHICKEN CHARDONNAY

| | |
|---|---|
| 2 | teaspoons canola oil |
| 4 | skinless chicken breast halves, cubed |
| | Salt & pepper to taste |
| ¼ | cup Chardonnay or other dry white wine |
| 1 | (14-ounce) can fat-free chicken broth |
| 1 | bay leaf |
| ¼ | teaspoon thyme |
| 1 | small onion, chopped |
| ½ | pound fresh mushrooms, sliced |
| ½ | cup fat-free sour cream |
| | Fresh parsley to garnish |

In a non-stick pan, heat 1 teaspoon canola oil and saute chicken cubes until lightly browned. Season to taste with salt and pepper. Add wine and cook until it is absorbed. Add chicken broth, bay leaf and thyme. Simmer on low for 20 minutes, or until chicken is tender.

In a separate saute pan, add the second teaspoon of oil. Saute the onions and mushrooms, until they are starting to brown. Add the vegetables and the sour cream to the chicken, blending well. Season again to taste with salt and pepper. Garnish with fresh parsley and serve over rice or noodles. Yield: 4 servings.

## Nutrition Facts

Per serving: Calories 160 (24% calories from fat)  Fat 4 g (saturated fat .6 g) Protein 19 g  Carbohydrates 10 g  Fiber 1 g  Cholesterol 39 mg  Sodium 425 mg.

*Poultry skin is high in saturated fat.  It's best to cook poultry with the skin on for moisture and flavor, but to remove it before serving.*

# CHICKEN IN SHERRY SAUCE

| | |
|---|---|
| 4 | chicken leg and thigh sections, skin removed |
| 1 | teaspoon salt |
| ¼ | teaspoon pepper |
| 1 | slice bacon |
| 1 | large onion, chopped |
| 4 | carrots, sliced |
| ½ | green pepper, chopped |
| 1 | cup consommé |
| 2 | teaspoons curry powder |
| ½ | cup dry sherry |
| 3 | cups cooked brown rice |

Season chicken with salt and pepper. Place chicken in a baking pan under the broiler until it browns.

Spray a non-stick skillet with vegetable cooking spray. Heat over medium-high, add bacon and cook until it crisps. Remove bacon and set aside to cool; then crumble. Sauté the onion, carrot and green pepper in the bacon drippings until they are lightly browned. Add consomme' and curry powder; simmer 10 minutes. Pour sauce over chicken in baking pan, reduce oven to 350° and bake chicken about 30 minutes. Add sherry and crumbled bacon bits and bake 30 minutes more. Serve chicken over rice with vegetables and sauce on top. Serves 4.

## Nutrition Facts

Per serving: Calories 439 (18% calories from fat) Fat 8.7 g (saturated fat 2.5 g) Protein 35 g Carbohydrates 45 g Fiber 5 g Cholesterol 108 mg Sodium 1287 mg.

# CLASSIC BBQ SAUCE

| | |
|---|---|
| 1 | cup tomato sauce |
| ½ | cup water |
| ¼ | cup vinegar |
| ¼ | cup catsup |
| 2 | tablespoons Worcestershire sauce |
| 1 | tablespoon paprika |
| 1 | teaspoon brown sugar |
| 1 | teaspoon dry mustard |
| ½ | teaspoon chili powder |
| ⅛ | teaspoon cayenne pepper |
| ⅛ | teaspoon lemon juice |
| 2 | cloves |
| 1 | bay leaf |
| | Dash Tabasco sauce |

Combine all ingredients and simmer for 15 minutes. Remove bay leaf and cloves before using. Use on grilled chicken, beef or pork. This recipe may be used as a marinade or a grilling sauce and is very good when combined with hickory wood. Yield: 1 ¾ cups or 16 servings.

## Nutrition Facts

Per serving: Calories 13 (16% calories from fat) Fat .1 g (saturated fat 0) Protein .4 g Carbohydrates 3 g Fiber .4 g Choldesterol 0 Sodium 160 mg.

*Marinades add tenderness and flavor to meats, poultry and seafood. They are always recommended when grilling to prevent food from becoming dry.*

# LEMON-HERB & HONEY GRILLED CHICKEN

| | |
|---|---|
| ⅓ | cup honey |
| ¼ | cup lemon juice |
| 2 | teaspoon dried rosemary leaves, crushed |
| ¼ | teaspoon crushed red pepper |
| 6 | skinned and boned chicken breast halves |
| | Salt and pepper to taste |

In a medium mixing bowl, combine honey, lemon juice, rosemary, red pepper and whisk together. Brush half of marinade on chicken and allow to stand for 15 minutes.

Heat grill to medium-hot heat and spray grill grids with non-stick cooking spray. Grill chicken breasts, covered with grill lid, 6 minutes on each side, (or until done) brushing with remaining marinade halfway through cooking time. Season with salt and pepper as desired. Yield: 6 servings.

NOTE: Try this recipe with other herbs such as tarragon, thyme, oregano or marjoram in place of the rosemary, for a totally different flavor.

## Nutrition Facts

Per serving: Calories 228 (8% calories from fat) Fat 2 g (saturated fat .5 g) Protein 35 g Carbohydrates 17 g Fiber .3 g Cholesterol 88 mg Sodium 99 mg.

# LIGHTHOUSE POINT LAMB RAGOUT WITH CURRY

| | |
|---|---|
| 1 | pound lean lamb meat, cut into 1-inch cubes |
| 1 | tablespoon canola oil |
| ½ | teaspoon sage |
| 1 | tablespoon grated lemon peel |
| 1 | medium chopped onion |
| 2 | cups beef bouillon |
| 1 | tablespoon curry powder |
| ½ | teaspoon salt |
| ⅛ | teaspoon pepper |
| 1 | green bell pepper, cut into strips |
| 1 | cup fresh mushrooms, sliced |
| 2 | tomatoes, peeled and quartered |
| 1 | tart apple, coarsely chopped |
| ½ | cup plain yogurt |

Heat oil in a heavy saucepan or Dutch oven. Add meat, sage and lemon rind and cook until meat is brown on all sides. Add onion, sauté lightly, then add bouillon and simmer about 50 minutes. Season with curry, salt and pepper. Add green pepper and simmer uncovered for 5 minutes. Stir in mushrooms, tomatoes and apple; simmer 5 minutes more. Remove from heat and cool mixture slightly. Stir in yogurt and serve at once. (Note: If additional heating is necessary, do not bring to a boil). Yield: 4 servings.

## Nutrition Facts

Per serving: Calories 242 (33% calories from fat) Fat 9 g (saturated 2.4 g) Protein 21 g Carbohydrates 20 g Fiber 4 g Cholesterol 51 mg Sodium 1341 mg.

*Buy lean meats and trim all visible fat away before cooking, to reduce fat intake.*

# MESQUITE-SMOKED TURKEY BREAST

| | |
|---|---|
| 2 | tablespoons chili powder |
| 1 | tablespoon paprika |
| 1 | teaspoon dried cumin |
| ½ | teaspoon garlic powder |
| ¼ | teaspoon dried red pepper |
| ⅛ | teaspoon salt |
| 1 | 6-pound turkey breast, skinned |
| | Vegetable cooking spray |
| | Mesquite chips |

Soak mesquite chips in water for 30 minutes, then drain. In the meantime, prepare the seasoning blend. Combine the chili powder, paprika, cumin, garlic powder, red pepper and salt in a small bowl. Whisk all together. Rinse turkey breast under cold tap water, and pat dry with paper towels. Rub seasoning mix inside and outside of turkey breast.

Preheat gas grill to medium-hot (350-400°) using both burners, then turn the left burner off. Place mesquite chips in a disposable aluminum foil pan (or an aluminum foil packet poked with holes) on grill over right burner. Coat grill rack with cooking spray; place on grill over medium-hot coals.

Insert meat thermometer into thickest part of turkey, making sure it does not touch bone. Place turkey on rack over left burner. Cook, covered, 3 hours or until meat thermometer registers 170°. Let stand 20 minutes before carving. Yield: 12 servings.

## Nutrition Facts

Per serving: Calories 273 (6% calories from fat) Fat 2 g (saturated fat .5 g) Protein 60 g Carbohydrates 1 g Fiber .6 g Cholesterol 177 mg Sodium 139 mg.

*A dry rub is a mixture of herbs and spices, and is recommended for coating tender cuts of meat, poultry and fish. Make your own, or buy them ready-made. A favorite is lemon- pepper.*

# NEW LONDON CHICKEN WITH MUSHROOMS & TARRAGON

6    boneless, skinless chicken breast halves
2    teaspoons olive oil
3    slices turkey bacon, sliced
8    ounces fresh mushrooms, thinly sliced
½    cup dry white wine
2    tablespoons tomato paste
1    teaspoon dried tarragon
⅔    cup fat-free half & half
1    teaspoon corn starch
2    scallions, finely chopped
     Salt and pepper to taste
     Fresh tarragon sprig for garnish (optional)

Heat a large non-stick skillet over medium-high heat. Spray with vegetable cooking spray. Add olive oil and sauté chicken breasts 2 minutes on each side, or until they brown. Remove chicken from skillet and place in a shallow baking dish; set aside.

Add the bacon to the pan and cook over medium-high heat 2 minutes, or until brown. Add the mushrooms and cook for 5 minutes. Add the wine, tomato paste and tarragon to the pan. Stir until the mixture boils. Combine the half & half and cornstarch in a measuring cup and stir to blend. Stir this mixture into the pan and simmer for 2 minutes. Remove from heat, stir in the scallions and season to taste with salt and pepper. Pour sauce over chicken and bake, covered in a pre-heated 350° oven for 20-30 minutes, until the chicken is tender. Chicken dish may be prepared ahead and refrigerated prior to baking, until ready to serve. Garnish with fresh tarragon sprig. Yield: 6 servings.

## Nutrition Facts

Per serving: Calories 181 (16% calories from fat) Fat 3 g (saturated .6 g) Protein 28 g Carbohydrates 5.4 g Fiber .8 g Cholesterol 66 mg Sodium 98 mg.

# NEWPORT HONEY BARBEQUED BROILERS

| | |
|---|---|
| 1 | 2 ½ - 3 pound whole broiler chicken |
| 3 | cloves garlic, minced |
| 1 ½ | teaspoons dried marjoram |
| 1 | teaspoon dry mustard |
| ½ | teaspoon salt |
| ½ | teaspoon black pepper |
| 2 | tablespoons honey |
| 2 | tablespoons balsamic vinegar |

Using a good boning knife, quarter the chicken, leaving skin in tact and discarding the back parts. Rinse quarters and pat dry with paper towels. Set aside.

In a small mixing bowl, combine garlic, marjoram, mustard, salt and pepper, honey and vinegar. Brush over entire surface of chicken pieces. Cover chicken and refrigerate at least 2 hours.

Place chicken quarters in a baking pan sprayed with non-stick cooking spray and bake in a 350° oven for 40 minutes to pre-cook. During this time, prepare a grill to medium-high heat. Remove chicken from oven, retaining juices in the pan. Grill for 15-20 minutes, or until done, turning once and basting with the pan juices. To serve, remove skin and place on individual serving plates. (Chicken may be served with skin, but will add extra fat to the recipe.) Yield: 4 servings.

NOTE: This recipe may be cooked to the end in the oven, if desired. The grilling adds the finishing smoky flavor.

## Nutrition Facts

Per serving: Calories 284 (29% calories from fat) Fat 8.8 g (saturated 2.3 g) Protein 38.4 g Carbohydrates 11 g Fiber .3 g Cholesterol 133 mg Sodium 144 mg.

# NORTH CAROLINA-STYLE PORK BARBECUE

1     3-pound loin of pork roast
1 ½   cups white vinegar
½     cup water
1     tablespoon hot pepper sauce
2     teaspoons prepared yellow mustard
1     teaspoon salt

To bake: heat oven to 400°. Place roast in baking pan and cover with aluminum foil. Bake in 400° for 30 minutes; reduce oven temperature to 325°. Bake another 3 hours or until fork slips easily into meat. When cool enough to handle, shred meat and place in a bowl.

To grill: prepare gas grill. Turn half of grill on high, leaving the other half off. Add water-soaked mesquite or hickory chips to side that is turned on. Place roast on side that is turned off. Grill, covered, until fork slips easily into meat and instant-read thermometer placed in thickest part of roast reads 170°. (This should take about 2 hours). Cook slowly, so meat does not burn on outside. When meat is cool enough to handle, shred and place in a bowl.

When pork is cooked and ready to serve, stir together vinegar, water, hot sauce, mustard and salt in a medium bowl. Stir half of vinegar mixture into shredded meat. Serve on split buns with remaining sauce on side. Yield: 12 servings.

Note: This recipe served with home-style coleslaw is a crowd pleaser and a real tradition on the beaches in North Carolina.

## Nutrition Facts

Per serving:  Calories 322 (41% calories from fat)  Fat 14 g (saturated fat 5 g)
Protein 22 g  Carbohydrates 24 g  Fiber .1 g  Cholesterol 71 mg  Sodium 316 mg.

*Hot pepper sauce has no calories or fat when used in small amounts. Besides zapping food with  flavor, it reduces the need for salt.*

# PAN-SEARED PORK WITH APPLES AND LEEKS

| | |
|---|---|
| 1 ½ | pounds boneless pork loin roast, sliced into 6 pieces |
| | Salt and pepper to taste |
| 3 | tablespoons cider vinegar |
| 2 | tablespoons sugar |
| ¾ | cup fat-free chicken broth |
| ½ | cup dry sherry |
| 1 | large apple, peeled, cored and thinly sliced |
| ½ | cup chopped leeks |
| 1 | tablespoon cornstarch dissolved in 1 tablespoon water |
| 2 | tablespoons fresh chopped parsley |

Heat a large non-stick skillet over medium heat and spray with non-stick cooking spray. Add the pork and cook for 5 minutes on each side. Season with salt and pepper. Remove the pork from the pan and set aside.

Add the vinegar and using a spatula, stir to de-glaze the pan. Add the sugar and stir until it dissolves. Pour in the broth and sherry, and bring to a boil. Add the apples and leeks and cook for about 3 minutes or until apples have softened. Add the cornstarch mixture, stir, then add the pork back into the pan and heat through. Serve the pork with the apple and leek sauce, and garnish with fresh parsley. Yield: 6 servings.

## Nutrition Facts

Per serving: Calories 227 (26% calories from fat)  Fat 6.5 g (saturated fat 2.2 g) Protein 25 g  Carbohydrates 13 g  Fiber 1 g  Cholesterol 65 mg  Sodium 85 mg.

*To sauté the healthy way, spray a cool non-stick skillet with veg-etable-cooking spray, heat, then add 1/4 the amount of oil called for in the recipe. Proceed with directions.*

# PENSACOLA PORK WITH CURRY & RICE

| ½ | tablespoon peanut oil |
|---|---|
| 1 | pound boneless pork chops or tenderloins |
| 2 | medium onions, sliced |
| 4 | small garlic cloves (or 3 large), minced |
| 1 | tablespoon lite soy sauce |
| 1 | teaspoon curry powder |
| 1 ½ | teaspoons chili powder |
| ¾ | teaspoon ground turmeric |
| ½ | teaspoon ginger |
| ⅓ | cup water |

In a medium saucepan, heat the peanut oil over medium heat. Add the pork and brown on both sides. Remove pork from saucepan and set aside. Add the onions to the pan juices and saute for 2 minutes, then add the garlic. Cook about 2 minutes more or until vegetables turn clear. Add soy sauce and spices, water and stir. Add pork back to saucepan, and gently blend all ingredients to distribute flavors. Turn heat to low and simmer 1 to 1 ½ hours or until pork is fork-tender. Serve over cooked white or brown rice. Yield: 4 servings.

## Nutrition Facts

Per serving:  Calories 209 (35% calories from fat)  Fat 8 g (saturated fat 2.4 g) Protein 26 g  Carbohydrates 7 g  Fiber 1.7 g  Cholesterol 62 mg  Sodium 196 mg.

# PORK TENDERLOIN IN CORIANDER PLUM SAUCE

| | |
|---|---|
| 1 | pound pork tenderloin |
| ½ | cup red wine |
| 2 | teaspoons olive oil |
| | Salt and pepper to taste |
| 1 | teaspoon coriander seeds |
| ⅓ | cup plum jam |

Marinate the pork in red wine and 1 teaspoon of olive oil, by placing all in a plastic zip-lock bag and refrigerating about 2 hours. Remove pork and reserve marinade. Season pork with salt and pepper to taste and set aside. Prepare and pre-heat grill.

Heat a non stick skillet to medium, then add the remaining 1 teaspoon of olive oil. Sauté the coriander seeds until fragrant. Add the marinade, deglaze the pan, then heat until marinade thickens. Add the plum jam, simmer on low for 2 minutes and remove from heat.

Baste pork with marinade and grill on medium for about 30 minutes or until done, turning and basting one more time. Slice tenderloin into ½-inch slices, arrange on a serving dish and spoon remaining marinade over slices. Serve immediately. Yield: 4 servings.

## Nutrition Facts

Per serving: Calories 203 (38% calories from fat)  Fat 8.5 g (saturated fat 2.4 g)
Protein 23 g  Carbohydrates 2.5 g  Fiber .3 g  Cholesterol 74 mg  Sodium 70 mg.

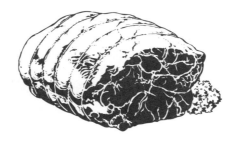

# SAN DIEGO STEAK SPANISH-STYLE

| | |
|---|---|
| 3 | pounds round steak, cut ½" thick |
| | Freshly ground pepper |
| 1 | clove garlic, minced |
| 2 | teaspoons salt |
| ½ | cup all-purpose flour |
| 1 | tablespoon olive oil |
| 2 | large tomatoes, peeled, seeded and chopped |
| 1 | small green bell pepper, chopped |
| 1 | medium onion, chopped |
| 1 | stalk celery, chopped |
| | Few sprigs parsley, minced |
| ½ | teaspoon sugar |
| ¼ | cup dry red wine |
| 2 | tablespoons water |
| 1-2 | tablespoons all-purpose flour |
| ½ | cup plain yogurt at room temperature |

Cut meat into serving pieces. Rub with freshly ground pepper and garlic. Sprinkle with salt and dredge in flour. Heat a heavy non-stick skillet and spray with vegetable cooking spray. Add olive oil, heat to medium, then add meat. Brown slowly on both sides. Mix tomatoes, green pepper, onion, celery, parsley, sugar and wine. Pour over meat. Cover and simmer 2 hours until meat is tender.

With a slotted spoon, remove meat to a serving platter. Add water to flour to make a smooth paste, and blend into sauce in skillet. Cook about 5 minutes, stirring constantly until thickened. Remove from heat. Stir yogurt until creamy and add gradually into hot sauce. Pour over steak and serve over hot steamed rice. Yield: 8 servings.

## Nutrition Facts

Per serving:  Calories 376 (42% calories from fat)  Fat 17 g (saturated fat 7 g)
Protein 39 g Carbohydrates 13 g Fiber 1.4 g Cholesterol 209 mg Sodium 687 mg.

*Meat & Poultry*

# SAUSAGE & PEPPER GRILL OVER RICE

| | |
|---|---|
| 1 | pound (hot or mild) Italian pork sausage |
| ⅓ | cup balsamic vinegar |
| 1 | teaspoon brown sugar |
| 1 | teaspoon olive oil |
| ½ | teaspoon salt |
| ¼ | teaspoon black pepper |
| 1 | sweet red bell pepper |
| 2 | green bell peppers |
| 2 | red onions |
| 4 | cups cooked, white rice |

Cut sausages into 24 pieces about 1-inch in length. Place in a saucepan and cover with water. Bring to a boil and simmer about 5 minutes to par-cook and remove fat. Set aside.

Heat grill to medium-hot (350-400°). Soak 12 wooden skewers in water and set aside. In a small mixing bowl, combine vinegar, brown sugar, olive oil, salt and pepper and set aside.

Cut each pepper into 4 strips. Remove stem and seeds, rinse and cut each strip in half again. (You will have 24 pieces of pepper). Remove the outer skin of the red onions and cut into 6 wedges each. You are now ready to assemble the skewers. Using 2 pieces of sausage, 3 pieces of assorted colored peppers and 1 wedge of red onion, thread 12 (moistened) skewers in any order you prefer. Place filled skewers on hot grill and cook 15 minutes, or until done, turning occasionally and brushing with balsamic mixture during the last 3 minutes of cooking. Transfer two skewers on individual serving plates, each filled with ¾ cup of rice. Use any remaining balsamic mixture to brush one more time. Serve immediately. Yield: 6 servings.

## Nutrition Facts

Per serving:  Calories 315 (32% calories from fat)  Fat 11 g (saturated fat 3.7 g)
Protein 12 g  Carbohydrates 41 g  Fiber 2.4 g  Cholesterol 30 mg  Sodium 556 mg.

*Meat & Poultry*

# SESAME GRILLED CHICKEN OVER A BED OF GREENS

| | |
|---|---|
| 1 | teaspoon vegetable oil |
| 2 | tablespoons white vinegar |
| 1 | tablespoon toasted sesame seeds |
| ½ | teaspoon sugar |
| 1 | teaspoon sesame oil |
| 4 | boneless, skinless chicken breast halves |
| 4 | cups mixed salad greens, cleaned |
| ½ | cup favorite low-fat salad dressing |
| | Alfalfa sprouts for garnish (optional) |

Mix vegetable oil, vinegar, sesame seeds, sugar and sesame oil together in a small bowl. Whisk together until well blended. Add chicken breasts and let marinate for 30 minutes. Meanwhile, heat grill. Grill chicken 4 to 6 inches from medium heat about 20 minutes, basting occasionally and turning once. (Juices will run clear, when chicken is done). Remove from grill and allow to cool slightly. Prepare 4 bowls of mixed greens. Slice each chicken breast and place one breast on top of each bowl of greens. Add 2 tablespoons of favorite low-fat salad dressing, garnish if desired with sprouts and serve. Yield: 4 servings.

## Nutrition Facts

Per serving: Calories 206 (25% calories from fat)  Fat 5.5 g (saturated fat 1 g)
Protein 29 g  Carbohydrates 9 g  Fiber 1.7 g  Cholesterol 69 mg  Sodium 415 mg.

# SWEET SAUSAGE OVER PENNE
# WITH BROCCOLI SAUCE

| | |
|---|---|
| 2 | cups steamed chopped broccoli with ½ cup of cooking broth |
| 1 | tablespoon olive oil |
| ½ | Italian sweet sausage (about 4 links) |
| 1 | medium size shallot, chopped |
| 1 | clove garlic, minced |
| 1 | teaspoon Italian seasoning |
| | Salt and pepper to taste |
| ½ | cup white wine |
| 12 | ounces cooked penne pasta |
| | Parmesan cheese (optional) |

Heat olive oil in a non-stick skillet over medium heat. Remove the sausage meat from its casings and break up into chunks. Sauté the sausage meat for 2 to 3 minutes, or until it starts to brown. Add the shallot, cook for one minute, then add garlic and cook for one minute more. Sprinkle with seasoning and salt and pepper to taste. Add wine, scraping the bottom of pan to deglaze it. Add broccoli and cooking broth and cook for several minutes for the flavors to blend and the sauce to reduce. Remove from heat and toss over cooked penne pasta in a large serving bowl. Sprinkle with Parmesan cheese, if desired and serve. Yield: 6 servings.

## Nutrition Facts

Per serving: Calories 398 (34% calories from fat) Fat 15 g (saturated fat 4.6g) Protein 18 g Carbohydrates 45.5g Fiber 3.5 g Cholesterol 35 mg Sodium 428.5 mg.

# TEXAS CHILI

| | |
|---|---|
| 1 | pound lean ground beef |
| 1 | medium onion, chopped |
| ¾ | cup water |
| 1 | (16-ounce) can pinto beans |
| 1 | tablespoon ketchup |
| 1 | teaspoon chili powder (more if desired) |
| ½ | teaspoon cumin |
| ¼ | teaspoon garlic powder |
| | Tabasco sauce to taste |
| ½ | cup plain low-fat yogurt at room temperature |
| 1 ½ | cups long-grain white rice, cooked according to package directions |

Spray a large heavy skillet with vegetable cooking spray and heat to medium-high temperature. Cook meat and onion, breaking meat up as you stir, until it is browned. Add water, pinto beans, ketchup, chili powder, cumin and garlic powder. Stir in desired amount of Tabasco sauce. Bring to a boil, reduce heat and simmer uncovered for 10 minutes.

In a small bowl, stir yogurt until creamy. Blend a small amount of hot chili into yogurt and gradually add chili-yogurt mixture back into the remaining chili. Serve immediately over hot steamed rice. Yield: 6 servings.

### Nutrition Facts

Per serving:  Calories 361 (35% calories from fat)  Fat 13.8 g (saturated fat 5.3 g)
Protein 21 g  Carbohydrates 37 g  Fiber 4.7 g  Cholesterol 52 mg  Sodium 340 mg.

*After browning meat for soups and stews, pour off as much fat as possible, before proceeding with the recipe.*

# VEGGIE BEEF BURGERS

| | |
|---|---|
| ½ | cup chopped onions |
| ½ | cup grated cabbage |
| 1 | carrot, peeled and grated |
| 1 | tablespoon chicken broth or white wine |
| ½ | cup uncooked oatmeal cereal |
| 2 | tablespoons smoky BBQ sauce |
| ¾ | pound lean ground beef (9% fat) |
| | Salt and pepper to taste |

Prepare a non-stick skillet with vegetable cooking spray. Heat to medium and add onion, cabbage and carrots. Cook about 2 minutes, or just until vegetables soften, then add chicken broth or wine, cooking one minute more. Stir in oatmeal, until it is moistened, then remove mixture from heat and cool.

In a separate mixing bowl, blend beef, BBQ sauce and cooled vegetable-oatmeal mixture with a wooden spoon. Season with salt and pepper to taste. Shape into five burgers and cook on a pre-heated grill for 5 minutes on one side, then turn and cook to desired degree of doneness. Yield: 5 servings.

## Nutrition Facts

Per serving:  Calories 151 (39% calories from fat)  Fat 6.4 g (saturated fat 2.5 g)
Protein 16 g  Carbohydrates 6 g  Fiber .8 g  Cholesterol 25 mg  Sodium 159 mg.

# VERO BEACH VEAL STEW WITH LEMON & BASIL

| | |
|---|---|
| 1 | pound lean veal shoulder |
| 1 | tablespoon canola oil |
| 1 | onion, chopped |
| ¼ | cup chopped carrots |
| ¼ | cup chopped celery |
| 2 | cloves garlic, chopped |
| ½ | cup red wine |
| 1 | tablespoon grated fresh lemon peel |
| 1 | tablespoon fresh basil, chopped |
| ½ | teaspoon salt |
| ⅛ | teaspoon pepper |
| 1 | large bell pepper, cut into wedges |
| 8 | ounces fresh mushrooms, sliced |
| 1 | (15-ounce) can crushed tomatoes |
| ¼ | cup fresh parsley, chopped |

Trim the excess fat from veal and cut it into 1-inch pieces. Heat oil in a heavy saucepan or Dutch oven over medium-high heat. Add veal, onion, carrots, celery and garlic. Cook 3 to 4 minutes stirring, until veal is browned. Stir in wine, lemon peel, basil, seasonings, bell pepper, mushrooms and tomatoes; bring mixture to a boil. Reduce heat and simmer for 50 to 60 minutes, stirring occasionally, until veal is tender. Just before serving, add parsley and enjoy. Yield: 4 servings.

NOTE: This dish goes well with steamed spinach and orzo.

## Nutrition Facts

Per serving: Calories 243 (27% calories from fat) Fat 7.4 g (saturated fat 1.4 g) Protein 25 g Carbohydrates 14 g Fiber 3 g Cholesterol 102 mg Sodium 482 mg.

*The illustrious lemon is loved by professional chefs for it's flavor and usefulness. It flavors vegetables without the fat and reduces the need for salt in savory dishes.*

# Fish & Shellfish

# Fish & Shellfish

# BAKED FLOUNDER WITH TOMATO SHERRY CREAM SAUCE

| | |
|---|---|
| 2 | garlic cloves, minced |
| 1 | tablespoon olive oil |
| ½ | cup sun-dried tomatoes (about 1 ounce) |
| ½ | cup water |
| 1 | tablespoon cornstarch |
| 2 | cups fat-free non-dairy creamer |
| ½ | cup dry sherry or white wine |
| 1 | teaspoon fresh chopped basil or ½ teaspoon dried |
| 6 | serving-size pieces flounder fillets |
| | Salt and pepper to taste |
| 2 | tablespoons chopped parsley |

Pre-heat oven to 350°. In a small saucepan sauté garlic in the olive oil. Turn heat down and add sun-dried tomatoes, tossing to coat. Immediately add water, cover pan and steam 2 or 3 minutes, until tomatoes are hydrated and tender. At this point, remove saucepan from the heat, mash tomatoes and garlic with a wooden spoon to a pasty consistency. Return the pan to low heat and slowly add the cornstarch to blend. Stir in the creamer, stirring until mixture thickens to desired consistency. Stir in sherry and basil and set aside. (Sauce may be thinned with additional sherry).

Spray a glass baking dish with vegetable cooking spray. Place fish fillets in a single layer into a baking dish. Season with salt and pepper to taste. Cover each flounder with equal amount of tomato cream sauce. Bake in oven 25 to 30 minutes or until fish flakes. Garnish with parsley and serve. Yield: 6 servings.

NOTE: This sauce may be used over other fish and shellfish as well as flounder.

## Nutrition Facts

Per serving: Calories 256 (16% calories from fat) Fat 4.3 g (saturated .8 g) Protein 35 g Carbohydrates 14 g Fiber .6 g Cholesterol 75 mg Sodium 321 mg.

# BOSTON SEA SCALLOPS

1    pound sea scallops
2    teaspoons olive oil
1    clove garlic, minced
3    tablespoons white wine
2    tablespoons fresh chopped parsley
     Lemon wedges
     Salt and pepper to taste

Remove scallops from store package and rinse in cold water. Pat dry with a paper towel and set aside.

Heat a non-stick skillet over medium heat. Add olive oil to heat, then add garlic. Sauté until garlic is light brown. Add scallops and cook over medium heat for 3-4 minutes, stirring constantly. Add wine and cook about 2 minutes more. This will deglaze the pan and add flavor to the scallops. Add parsley, salt and pepper to taste. Remove to a serving dish and garnish with lemon wedges. Serves 4.

## Nutrition Facts

Per serving:  Calories 129 (23% calories from fat)  Fat 3 g (saturated .4 g)  Protein 19 g  Carbohydrates 3 g  Fiber 0  Cholesterol 37 mg  Sodium 184 mg.

# BOUILLABAISSE VILLAGE-STYLE

| | |
|---|---|
| 1 | pound red snapper |
| 2 | medium lobster tails |
| ¼ | cup olive oil |
| 1 | cup sliced leeks |
| 1 | cup sliced onions |
| 4 | cloves garlic, minced |
| 4 | cups crushed tomatoes |
| 1 | bay leaf |
| ¼ | teaspoon saffron strands |
| ½ | teaspoon thyme |
| ½ | teaspoon pepper sauce |
| 2 | teaspoons salt |
| ½ | teaspoon black pepper |
| ½ | cup dry white wine |
| 12 | large clams, scrubbed well |
| 1 | pound large shrimp, peeled and deveined |
| 8 | slices French bread, toasted |
| ¼ | cup chopped fresh parsley |

Have snapper well cleaned and cut into slices 2 inches thick. Cut each lobster tail into 4 sections. Set aside.

Pour oil into a large Dutch oven over medium-high heat. When hot, sauté leeks and onions for 2 minutes. Add garlic and cook one minute more. Add tomatoes, bay leaf, saffron, thyme, pepper sauce, salt and pepper. Stir gently and simmer over low heat 20-30 minutes.

Place lobster pieces into sauce, add fish, making sure all seafood is covered with sauce. Simmer gently for about 8 minutes. Pour in wine, add clams and shrimp, cooking another 5-8 minutes, or until shrimp turn pink and all clam shells are open. Discard any that do not.

Place toasted French bread into large soup bowls; spoon seafood onto toast, cover with sauce, sprinkle with parsley and serve piping hot. Yield: 8 servings.

## Nutrition Facts

Per serving: Calories 419 (30% calories from fat) Fat 14 g (saturated 2.8 g) Protein 39 g Carbohydrates 30 g Fiber 1.4 g Cholesterol 166 mg Sodium 1027 mg.

*Fish & Shellfish*

# CALIFORNIA STUFFED CALAMARI

| | |
|---|---|
| 2 | medium tubes calamari |
| 1 | tablespoon olive oil |
| 2 | scallions, chopped |
| ½ | cup currants |
| 2 | tablespoons chopped fresh parsley |
| 2 | tablespoons grated lemon rind |
| 1 ½ | cups cooked rice |
| 1 | egg, slightly beaten |

## SAUCE:

| | |
|---|---|
| 1 | tablespoon olive oil |
| 1 | onion, finely chopped |
| 1 | clove garlic, crushed |
| 4 | large ripe tomatoes, peeled and chopped |
| ¼ | cup red wine |
| ½ | teaspoon oregano |

Wash and dry calamari tubes. Combine oil, scallions, currants, parsley, lemon rind and rice in a bowl. Toss to mix ingredients. Add enough beaten egg to moisten all. Fill each calamari tube three-quarters full, securing ends with a toothpick or skewer. Place in a single layer in a casserole dish sprayed with non-stick cooking spray.

To make sauce, heat oil in a medium saucepan. Add onion and garlic, cook over low heat until onion is soft (about 2 minutes). Add tomato, wine and oregano. Cover and cook over low heat for 10 minutes. Pour sauce over calamari; cover and bake in a pre-heated 325° oven for 20 minutes or until tender. Remove toothpicks, slice into thick slices, spoon sauce over slices and serve. Yield: 6 servings.

### Nutrition Facts

Per serving:  Calories 218 (28% calories from fat)  Fat 6.7 g (saturated fat 1.2 g
Protein 15 g  Carbohydrates 22 g  Fiber 2.3 g  Cholesterol 207 mg  Sodium 56 mg.

# CAPISTRANO SHORE'S CRISPY BAKED
# SEA TROUT

1     pound trout fillets, without skin
1     teaspoon canola oil
3     tablespoons flour
½    cup skim milk
2     ounces fat-free potato chips
      Lemon wedges (optional)

Prepare fish fillets by patting with a paper towel to dry excess moisture. Using a brush, lightly coat the fillets with oil. Place the flour in a shallow bowl and do the same with the milk. Crush the potato chips and place in a third shallow bowl.

Prepare a baking pan large enough to hold all fillets in one layer, by spraying with vegetable cooking spray. Dredge each fillet in flour, then dip into milk and dredge into the potato chips. Placed crusted fillets next to one another in the prepared baking pan and bake in a pre-heated 350° oven for fifteen minutes, or until fish is flaky and top is browned. Serve with lemon, if desired. Yield: 4 servings.

NOTE: This is a good recipe for flounder or any mild white and skinless fish.

## Nutrition Facts

Per serving: Calories 143 (22% calories from fat) Fat 3.5 g (saturated .7 g) Protein 13 g  Carbohydrates 15 g  Fiber .7 g  Cholesterol 51 mg  Sodium 151 mg.

*The "good fat diet" calls for substituting fat found in olive and canola oils, fish and seafood (especially salmon) for animal fat found in meat and dairy products.*

# CAPTAIN'S CRABMEAT THERMIDOR

| | |
|---|---|
| 1 | tablespoon butter |
| ¼ | cup chopped onion |
| ⅓ | cup green bell pepper, chopped |
| 1 | (10 ½ -ounce) can cream of potato soup |
| ½ | cup 1% milk |
| ½ | cup shredded Parmesan cheese |
| 1 | pound cooked crabmeat |
| 1 | tablespoon dry sherry wine |
| 3 | cups cooked rice |

Melt butter in a 2-quart saucepan. Sauté onion and pepper in butter until tender. Add soup, milk and cheese; heat and stir until blended. Fold in crabmeat and sherry, and heat thoroughly. Serve immediately over hot rice. Yield: 6 servings.

## Nutrition Facts

Per serving: Calories 229 (29% calories from fat)  Fat 7.4 g (saturated fat 4 g) Protein 22.5 g  Carbohydrates 17.5 g  Fiber .5 g  Cholesterol 75 mg  Sodium 879 mg.

# CHESAPEAKE COCONUT CRAB CAKES

| | |
|---|---|
| 1 | pound fresh lump crabmeat |
| ¼ | cup egg substitute (or egg whites) |
| ½ | cup finely crushed fat-free potato chips |
| 2 | tablespoons shredded coconut, toasted |
| 2 | tablespoons finely chopped green onion |
| 2 | tablespoons light mayonnaise |
| 1 | tablespoon fresh chopped parsley |
| ½ | teaspoon dried coriander |
| | Fresh lemon slices for garnish |

Carefully pick over the crab meat to assure all shell material has been removed; set aside. In a medium bowl, combine egg substitute, potato chips, coconut, green onion, mayonnaise, parsley and coriander. Stir in the crab meat and turn gently to blend, being careful not to break up large lumps of crab. Shape mixture into 8 patties about ½-inch thick. Place crab cakes on a baking sheet that has been sprayed with non-stick cooking spray. Lightly spray the tops of the patties. Broil about 6 inches under the heat until the top browns. Turn and brown the second side. This should take about 10 to 15 minutes. Serve immediately with fresh lemon wedges. Yield: 8 crabcakes.

## Nutrition Facts

Per serving: Calories 82 (21% calories from fat) Fat 2 g (saturated fat .7 g)
Protein 6 g Carbohydrates 10 g Fiber .7 g Cholesterol 16 mg Sodium 228 mg.

# DAYTONA BEACH DOLPHIN PICANTE

| | |
|---|---|
| 1 | teaspoon margarine |
| 1 | teaspoon Canola oil |
| 2 | teaspoons chili powder |
| 1 | medium red onion, chopped |
| 1 | clove garlic, crushed |
| 1 | medium whole tomato, chopped |
| 1 | cup chicken broth (more if needed) |
| | Juice of 1 lemon |

Heat a non-stick skillet over medium and add the margarine and oil. Add the chili powder and cook for about 2 minutes. Add the onion and garlic and cook 3 to 5 minutes. Add the tomato, chicken broth and lemon juice. Cover and simmer on low heat about 30 minutes or until the sauce is thick and creamy. You may add more chicken broth, if necessary. Place fish fillets directly into the sauce, being sure to cover the fish with the sauce. Season with salt and pepper to taste. Simmer fish covered for 10 minutes or until fish is done. Remove from heat and serve immediately. Yield: 4 servings

## Nutrition Facts

Per serving: Calories 140 (22% calories from fat)  Fat 3.4 g (saturated fat 17 g)
Protein 22 g  Carbohydrates 5 g  Fiber 1.3 g  Cholesterol 84 mg. Sodium 298 mg.

# DEWEY BEACH BARBECUED BLUEFISH

½   cup fresh lime juice
¼   cup cider vinegar
4   cloves garlic, crushed
2   tablespoons olive oil
2   teaspoons fresh ginger, minced
   Salt and pepper to taste
2   pounds bluefish steaks
   Fresh lime slices

To prepare marinade, combine lime juice, vinegar, garlic, olive oil, ginger, salt and pepper and whisk together to blend well. Set aside.

Rinse fish well and cut out the dark vein of meat that runs down the center of the steak. Place fish into a shallow glass dish; pour marinade over and refrigerate covered at least 3 hours, turning once to allow fish to absorb the flavors.

When ready to cook, prepare grill. Remove fish from marinade and reserve the marinade. Cook fish 10-12 minutes on the grill, turning once and brushing occasionally with reserved marinade. Fish will look lightly browned when done. Serve immediately with fresh lime slices. Yield: 6 servings.

NOTE: Try this recipe with other gamefish. The flavors will enhance tuna, swordfish, wahoo, dolphin, marlin, king mackerel, bass or any other.

## Nutrition Facts

Per serving:  Calories 237 (42% calories from fat)  Fat 11 g (saturated fat 2 g)
Protein 30 g  Carbohydrates 3 g  Fiber .2 g  Cholesterol 89 mg  Sodium 91 mg.

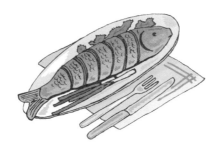

# EASTERN SHORE BROILED SOFT-SHELL CRABS

| | |
|---|---|
| 12 | soft-shell crabs, cleaned well |
| 1 | tablespoon butter, melted |
| 2 | tablespoons canola oil |
| 1 | teaspoon Old Bay seafood seasoning |
| 1 | teaspoon Worcestershire sauce |
| 1 | tablespoon fresh lemon juice |
| | Salt and pepper to taste |
| | Fresh chopped parsley for garnish |
| | Fresh lemon wedges |

Combine melted butter, canola oil, seafood seasoning, Worcestershire sauce and lemon juice in a small bowl. Using a basting brush, coat each crab with the mixture on both sides. Place crabs in a single layer, top side down, into a baking pan lined with foil. Season with salt and pepper as desired. Broil 5-6 inches under the heating element about 3 minutes, turn and broil 3 minutes on the other side, or until the soft-shells turn red Remove from oven, sprinkle with parsley and serve with lemon wedges. Yield: 6 servings.

## Nutrition Facts

Per serving:  Calories 181 (29% calories from fat)  Fat 6 g (saturated fat 1.4 g)
Protein 32 g  Carbohydrates .5 g  Fiber .1 g  Cholesterol 112 mg  Sodium 581 mg.

# FENWICK ISLAND FISH PATTIES

| | |
|---|---|
| 1 | pound fresh cooked mild, white fish (grouper, flounder, redfish, sea bass, snook or other) |
| 1 | small onion, grated or minced |
| ¼ | cup combined red and green bell pepper, finely chopped |
| 1 | egg, beaten |
| 2 | tablespoons whole mayonnaise |
| 1 | tablespoon fresh lemon juice |
| 1 | teaspoon lemon zest |
| 1 | teaspoon Cajun seasoning (or more to taste) |
| 1 | teaspoon Outerbridge's sherry pepper sauce or Worcestershire sauce |
| ½ | cup seasoned bread crumbs |
| 2 | tablespoons fresh chopped parsley |
| | Salt and pepper to taste |

Cut cooked fish into pieces and place in a food processor. Process quickly to shred and place shredded fish into a large bowl. Add onion, bell peppers, egg, mayonnaise, lemon juice and zest; toss gently to blend. Season with Cajun seasoning, Outerbridge's or Worcestershire sauce, seasoned breadcrumbs and parsley and toss once more. Add salt and pepper to taste. Form mixture into 8 patties and place on a foil-lined baking pan. Fish patties may be refrigerated at this point.

When ready to cook, preheat oven to 400°. Spray patties with vegetable cooking spray and bake for 15 minutes or until browned. These are great served with lemon slices and your favorite tartar sauce. Yield: 8 patties.

## Nutrition Facts

Per serving: Calories 138 (28% calories from fat) Fat 4.2 g (saturated fat .9 g) Protein 16 g Carbohydrates 8 g Fiber .9 g Cholesterol 48 mg Sodium 492 mg.

*Creating fried flavors with oven-baked foods is easy with vegetable cooking spray,. Simply coat the food with selected coating and spray the surface with cooking spray. Bake as directed. This hastens the cooking time, causing the coating to shrink around the food, seal in moisture and crisp the outside.*

# FLORIDA ROCK SHRIMP BROILED IN THE SHELL

| | |
|---|---|
| 1 | tablespoon canola oil |
| 1 | tablespoon lemon juice |
| 2 | tablespoons sherry |
| 3 | cloves garlic, minced |
| 1 | teaspoon paprika |
| ½ | teaspoon salt |
| 2 | pounds rock shrimp, in the shell |

Prepare a marinade by blending oil, lemon juice, sherry, garlic, paprika and salt in a small bowl. Whisk gently and set aside.

Clean the whole rock fish by placing on a cutting board, shell side down. With a sharp knife make a cut through the exposed underside. Spread the shell open until it lies flat, then wash with cold water to remove the vein.

Pre-heat the broiler and prepare a baking pan large enough to hold the rock shrimp. Lay them flat on the baking pan with the meat exposed. Using a basting brush, baste each rock shrimp with the marinade. Broil approximately 4 inches from the heat source for about 2 minutes, or until the tails turn up. (Be careful not to overcook, as rock fish will cook faster than other shrimp.) Serve immediately. Yield: 4 servings.

## Nutrition Facts

Per serving: Calories 123 (33% calories from fat) Fat 4.4 g (saturated fat .5 g) Protein 17.5 g Carbohydrates 1.5 g Fiber .2 g Cholesterol 161 mg Sodium 477 mg.

# FOLLY BEACH FLOUNDER WITH AVOCADO SAUCE

1 ½   pounds flounder fillets (4 pieces)
2   tablespoons 1% milk
¼   cup dry bread crumbs
1   tablespoon canola oil
1   large ripe avocado (1 cup mashed)
2   tablespoons juice and pulp of lime
1   garlic clove, minced
¼   teaspoon salt
⅛   teaspoon pepper
⅛   teaspoon cayenne pepper (optional)
⅛   teaspoon ground cumin (optional)
     Lime slices for garnish

Place flounder fillets on a flat plate and brush both sides with milk. Dredge fillets in bread crumbs on both sides. Heat a non-stick skillet over medium heat and coat bottom lightly with oil. Sauté flounder fillets about 3 minutes on first side, turn and lightly coat with oil if needed. Cook another 2-3 minutes (depending on the thickness of the fillets), or until fish is flaky. Remove cooked flounder to a baking dish and place in a 250° oven to keep warm.

Prepare the avocado sauce by scooping out the flesh of the avocado and mashing in a small mixing bowl with a fork. Add onions, garlic, lime juice and pulp, salt and pepper, blending all ingredients. Add cumin and cayenne pepper if desired. Stir once more to blend.

Remove warm fillets from the oven and place on each individual plate. Top each fillet with avocado sauce and serve. Garnish with lime slices if desired. Yield: 4 servings.

## Nutrition Facts

Per serving: Calories 322 (41% calories from fat) Fat 14.7 g (saturated 3.2 g)
Protein 34 g Carbohydrates 13 g Fiber 3.5 g Cholesterol 82 mg Sodium 352 mg.

*Fish and seafood are excellent sources of protein, vitamins and minerals; and are low in calories and saturated fat.*

# GULF SHORES BAKED GROUPER IN PARCHMENT

| | |
|---|---|
| 1 | tablespoon Canola oil |
| 2 | pounds grouper fillets |
| 12 | chopped scallions |
| 2 | chopped tomatoes |
| 1 | zucchini, thinly sliced |
| 1 | teaspoon oregano |
| | Salt and pepper to taste |
| | Juice of 2 lemons |
| 2 | tablespoons Parmesan cheese |

Pre-heat oven to 375°. Cut parchment paper or aluminum foil to wrap each fish fillet. Brush fish fillets with oil and place each one in the center of paper or foil wraps. Top each fillet with scallions, tomatoes and zucchini. Sprinkle with salt and pepper to taste, oregano and lemon juice. Top all off with Parmesan cheese and seal the package to completely enclose the fish. Place packages in a single layer on a cookie sheet and bake for 20 minutes. Check for doneness. Fish may be served in it's packet. Yield: 6 servings.

## Nutrition Facts

Per serving:  Calories 190 (23% calories from fat)  Fat 4.5 g (saturated fat 1 g)
Protein 31 g  Carbohydrates 4.7 g  Fiber 1.5 g  Cholesterol 58 mg  Sodium 89 mg.

## HAWAIIAN SWORDFISH WITH TOMATO-PAPAYA SALSA

| | |
|---|---|
| ¼ | cup fresh lime juice |
| ⅓ | cup fresh cilantro, divided |
| 2 | teaspoons olive oil |
| 4 | swordfish steaks (4½ x 2½ x ¾) |
| ⅜ | teaspoon salt, divided |
| ⅜ | teaspoon pepper, divided |
| | Vegetable cooking spray |
| 1 | cup diced tomato |
| 1 | cup diced papaya |
| 2 | tablespoons diced red onion |
| ½ | teaspoon sugar |
| ½ | teaspoon ground cumin |
| ⅛ | teaspoon hot pepper sauce |

Combine ¼ cup lime juice, 2 tablespoons cilantro and olive oil in a large shallow dish. Place the swordfish in the marinade and turn to coat. Cover and let stand in refrigerator for 20 minutes, turning once.

Meanwhile, prepare the salsa. In a medium bowl, combine the tomato, papaya, red onion, and remaining cilantro. Toss gently to mix. Add sugar, cumin, ⅛ teaspoon each of salt and pepper and the hot sauce, turning again gently to blend all ingredients. Let salsa set at room temperature.

Remove swordfish steaks from marinade, discarding marinade. Sprinkle with remaining salt and pepper and place fish in a grilling basket coated with vegetable cooking spray. Place on grill rack over medium-hot heat (350-400°). Grill, uncovered, approximately 12 minutes on each side, or until fish flakes easily when tested with a fork.

Transfer swordfish to a serving platter, and top evenly with tomato-papaya salsa. Sprinkle with remaining cilantro. Yield: 4 servings.

### Nutrition Facts

Per serving: Calories 220 (33% calories from Fat) Fat 8 g (saturated 2 g) Protein 28 g Carbohydrates 9 g Fiber 1.1 g Cholesterol 53 mg Sodium 133 mg.

## LAGUNA BEACH SNAPPER WITH BAY SHRIMP SAUCE

| | |
|---|---|
| 2 | tablespoons olive oil |
| 2 | celery stalks, chopped |
| 1 | medium onion, chopped |
| ½ | green bell pepper, chopped |
| 2 | garlic cloves, chopped |
| ¼ | teaspoon crushed red pepper |
| 1 | (14 ½-ounce) can Italian-style stewed tomatoes |
| ¼ | cup dry white wine |
| 2 | tablespoons tomato paste |
| 4 | (6-ounce) snapper fillets |
| | Salt and pepper to taste |
| 1 | tablespoon flour |
| ¼ | pound fresh bay shrimp, peeled and cleaned |

Heat 1 tablespoon olive oil in a heavy saucepan over medium heat. Add celery and onion and green pepper. Saute for 2 minutes, then add the garlic and red pepper, cooking two minutes more or until vegetables are soft. Stir in stewed tomatoes in their juices, wine and tomato paste. Simmer until sauce thickens, breaking up tomatoes, for about 10 minutes. Stir in bay shrimp, remove from heat and set aside.

Season fish with salt and pepper and coat with flour. Heat the remaining 1 tablespoon of olive oil in a non-stick skillet over medium heat. Add snapper to skillet and saute until brown, about 2 minutes each side. You may drizzle a little white wine into the skillet to deglaze the pan while the fish is cooking on the second side (optional). Top each fillet with shrimp and sauce: simmer on low heat just until fish is cooked through (about 10 minutes). Yield: 4 servings.

### Nutrition Facts

Per serving: Calories 336 (26% calories from fat) Fat 9.5 g (saturated fat 1.5 g)
Protein 43 g Carbohydrates 14 g Fiber 2.2 g Cholesterol 118 mg Sodium 432 mg.

# MAINE LOBSTER TAILS WITH SHERRY BUTTER SAUCE

| | |
|---|---|
| 4 | lobster tails (about 7 ounces each) |
| 1 | cup fat-free chicken broth |
| 2 | tablespoons unsalted butter |
| 1 | tablespoon fresh lemon juice |
| ½ | cup dry sherry wine |

Using kitchen shears, slice through the back hard shells of the lobster tails from one end to the other. (This will prevent them from curling as they cook). Prepare a grill or broiler at medium-high heat. Place lobster tails on grill or broiler pan cut-side down. Cook 5-7 minutes per side or until lobster meat is done. Do not overcook.

While lobster tails are cooking, prepare the sherry-butter sauce in a small saucepan. Heat the chicken broth to a simmer, then add the butter and allow it to melt. Stir in the lemon and sherry and return the mixture to a simmer once more. Remove from heat and pour into 4 individual dipping bowls. Serve lobster tails right off the grill or out of the broiler, dipping the succulent lobster into this extravagant, yet low-fat sauce. Yield: 4 servings.

## Nutrition Facts

Per serving:  Calories 206 (33% calories from fat)  Fat 13 g (saturated fat 7.5 g) Protein 51 g  Carbohydrates 3.5 g  Fiber 0  Cholesterol 206 mg  Sodium 989 mg.

*Fat contains more calories (9 per gram) than carbohydrates or protein (4 per gram). Reducing fat intake will decrease daily calorie total.*

# MALIBU STUFFED SHRIMP WITH CRAB MEAT

| | |
|---|---|
| 20 | extra-large shrimp or prawns, peeled and cleaned |
| 1 | pound fresh lump crabmeat |
| 1 | large egg |
| ¼ | cup finely chopped red pepper |
| ¼ | cup finely chopped green onion |
| 2 | tablespoon chopped parsley or cilantro |
| 2 | tablespoons low-fat mayonnaise |
| 2 | teaspoons Dijon mustard |
| 1 ½ | teaspoons crab-boil or seafood seasoning |
| ½ | teaspoon hot pepper sauce |
| ½ | teaspoon Worcestershire sauce |
| ⅔ | cups fresh fine bread crumbs |
| 2 | ounces grated Parmesan cheese |
| | Lemon wedges for garnish |

Butterfly shrimp by splitting down back of shrimp to within ½-inch of tail. Place butterflied shrimp on a baking pan that has been sprayed with non-stick cooking spray. Pick through crab meat to remove pieces of carti-lage.

In a large bowl, mix egg, pepper, scallions, parsley, mayonnaise, mustard, seasoning, pepper sauce and Worcestershire. Stir to blend ingredients. Add crab meat and breadcrumbs; gently stir to combine, trying not to break up large lumps of crab. (Mixture will be loose.) Place equal amounts (about 1-ounce) of crab meat on each butterflied shrimp. Sprinkle stuffed shrimp with Parmesan cheese. Place shrimp under the broiler and cook until they turn opaque and the surface browns, about 6 to 8 minutes. Garnish with lemon wedges and serve immediately. Yield: 4 servings.

NOTE: Try this same recipe with lobsters prepared for broiling.

## Nutrition Facts

Per serving:  Calories 267 (22% calories from fat)  Fat 6 g (saturated fat 1.7 g)
Protein 33.5 g Carbohydrates 17 g Fiber 1 g Cholesterol 212 mg Sodium 775 mg.

# MARCO ISLAND STEAMED SNOOK

4     (6-ounce) snook fillets
4     large fresh basil leaves
2     cloves garlic, minced
1     tablespoon shredded fresh ginger
2     cups thinly sliced sweet red and yellow peppers
1     pound asparagus spears

Prepare fish fillets by making shallow bias cuts ¾-inch apart on top side. Chop basil leaves and press into each cut. Rub fillets with minced garlic and ginger. Set aside.

Prepare a steamer basket by layering sweet peppers and asparagus on bottom, placing fish on top. Fill a large saucepan or wok with one inch of water and bring to a boil. Place steamer basket into pan and cover. Steam 6-8 minutes or until fish flakes easily with a fork. Remove fish fillets to four serving plates and top with vegetables. Yield: 4 servings.

### Nutrition Facts

Per serving: Calories 303 (28% calories from fat) Fat 9 g (saturated fat 2.2 g) Protein 42 g Carbohydrates 10.5 g Fiber 4 g Cholesterol 93 mg Sodium 68 mg.

# MARYLAND STEAMED BLUE CRABS

¼     cup seafood seasoning
¼     teaspoon salt
1 ½   cups white vinegar
1 ½   cups beer
18    live Maryland blue hardshell crabs

Prepare a large steaming pot with a rack on the bottom and a tight-fitting lid. Mix the seasoning and salt and set aside. Pour the vinegar and beer into the bottom of the steamer and bring the liquid to a boil. Place crabs into the pot of steaming water and pour seasoning over the top. Steam, covered, until the crabs turn bright red, about 20-30 minutes. Do not cook any crabs that are not moving. Serve immediately. Yield: 6 servings.

NOTE: Refrigerate leftover cooked crab to be picked for crabmeat for later use.

### Nutrition Facts

Per serving: Calories 113 (9% calories from fat) Fat 1 g (saturated fat .1 g) Protein 12 g Carbohydrates 5 g Fiber .6 g Cholesterol 49 mg Sodium 1236 mg.

# MISSION BEACH FILLET OF SOLE ALMONDINE

| | |
|---|---|
| 2 | teaspoons olive oil |
| 1 ½ | tablespoons sliced almonds |
| 1 ½ | tablespoons fresh lime juice |
| 2 | teaspoons grated lime rind |
| 4 | sole fillets (about 6-ounces each) |
| | Parsley or cilantro sprigs and lemon wedges for garnish |

Heat olive oil in a medium non-stick skillet, over medium heat. Add the almonds; cook, stirring constantly, until lightly browned. Remove the pan from the heat, stir in the lime juice and rind. Place mixture into a small bowl, leaving some of it on the pan surface. Place the skillet over medium heat and cook the sole fillets. Cook 2 minutes on each side or until done (fish will flake when touched with a fork). Carefully remove the fish fillets from the pan and place on serving plates. Top each fillet with the sautéed almond mixture. Garnish with cilantro or parsley and wedges of lime. Serve immediately. Yield: 4 servings.

## Nutrition Facts

Per serving: Calories 189 (27% calories from fat) Fat 5.5 g (saturated fat 1 g) Protein 32 g Carbohydrates 1 g Fiber .3 g Cholesterol 81 mg Sodium 137 mg.

*Brushing oil on a sauté pan with a pastry brush will guarantee complete coverage, while reducing the amount of oil used.*

*Fish & Shellfish*

# MONTEREY SHRIMP SCAMPI

| | |
|---|---|
| 1 | tablespoon butter |
| 1 | tablespoon olive oil |
| 4 | cloves garlic, minced |
| 1 | pound large shrimp, peeled and cleaned |
| ¼ | cup dry white wine |
| 1 | tablespoon fresh lemon juice |
| ½ | teaspoon salt |
| ⅛ | teaspoon pepper |
| 1 | tablespoon flavored bread crumbs |
| 2 | tablespoons Parmesan cheese |

Heat a large non-stick skillet over medium high heat. Add butter and olive oil. When butter melts and sizzles, add garlic and cook for 1 minute. Add shrimp and cook for 2 minutes; shrimp should only be partially cooked. Add wine, lemon juice, salt and pepper; cook about 2 minutes more until the shrimp are cooked through. (They will turn pink and the tails will curl). Remove from heat and top with bread crumbs and parsley. Place shrimp on serving plates, sprinkle with Parmesan cheese and serve immediately.

NOTE: This shrimp goes well tossed over cooked linguini.

## Nutrition Facts

Per serving: Calories 208 (40% calories from fat) Fat 9 g (saturated fat 3 g) Protein 24 g  Carbohydrates 4 g  Fiber .24 g  Cholesterol 182 mg  Sodium 424 mg.

# NANTUCKET COD BAKED WITH LEMON & VEGETABLES

| | |
|---|---|
| 6 | serving-size pieces cod (about 2 pounds total) |
| 2 | fresh lemons, sliced thinly |
| 1 | tablespoon olive oil |
| | Salt and pepper to taste |
| 6 | chopped scallions |
| 2 | chopped tomatoes |
| 1 | zucchini, thinly sliced |
| 1 | teaspoon oregano |
| 2 | tablespoons Parmesan cheese |

Cut 6 pieces of parchment paper (or foil) large enough to enclose each piece of fish. Line each piece of parchment with lemon slices. Brush cod fillets on both sides with olive oil. Place one fillet on center of each piece of parchment paper and season with salt and pepper as desired. Top with scallions, tomato and zucchini. Sprinkle with oregano and Parmesan cheese. Seal the packet to completely enclose the fish. Place packets in a single layer on a cookie sheet and bake for 20 minutes, or until fish is light and flaky. Fish may be served in it's package. Yield: 6 servings.

## Nutrition Facts

Per serving: Calories 172 (22% calories from fat) Fat 4 g (saturated fat 1 g) Protein 28 g  Carbohydrates 5 g  Fiber 1.3 g  Cholesterol 66 mg  Sodium 126 mg.

# NAUSET BEACH MUSSELS AND CLAMS MARINARA

| | |
|---|---|
| 2 | tablespoons olive oil |
| 2 | shallots chopped |
| 2 | cloves garlic, minced |
| ⅔ | cup white wine |
| 1 | (28-ounce) can Italian peeled tomatoes |
| 2 | tablespoons fresh lemon zest |
| 2 | tablespoons capers, drained and chopped |
| 1 | teaspoon salt |
| ½ | teaspoon pepper |
| 24 | medium-size raw clams |
| 12 | large mussels |
| 1 | tablespoon butter |
| ¼ | cup chopped fresh parsley |
| 1 | (8-ounce) package spaghetti or other favorite pasta |

In a large Dutch oven, heat the oil over medium heat. Add shallots and garlic and cook until the shallots are clear and the garlic turns light brown. Add wine, tomatoes, lemon zest and capers. Bring all to a slow simmer and season with salt and pepper. Add clams and mussels and cook until all shellfish have opened. (This should take about 10-15 minutes). Discard any clams or mussels that have not opened. Add butter to the sauce and let it melt on top. Add about half or 2 tablespoons of parsley and save the remainder for a garnish.

In a large saucepan, cook spaghetti or pasta according to package directions. When spaghetti is done serve it up equally into 4 pasta bowls. Give the clams and mussels marinara sauce a gentle turn to mix in the melted butter, and ladle into the bowls. Garnish with remaining parsley. Yield: 4 servings.

## Nutrition Facts

Per serving:  Calories 377 (30% calories from fat)  Fat 12 g (saturated fat 3 g)
Protein 25 g  Carbohydrates 32 g  Fiber 3.5 g  Cholesterol 54 mg  Sodium 1352 mg.

# NEW ENGLAND FISH & CHIPS

| | |
|---|---|
| 4 | serving-size pieces cod fillet |
| 1 | tablespoon lite mayonnaise |
| ¼ | cup crushed potato chips (fat-free) |
| ¼ | cup dry plain bread crumbs |
| 2 | teaspoons paprika |
| 4 | medium-size potatoes |
| 1 | tablespoon canola oil |
| 1 | teaspoon salt |
| | Malt vinegar (optional) |

Prepare cod fillets by blotting with a paper towel to insure a dry surface. Spread a thincoat of mayonnaise over both sides of fish: set aside. In a medium shallow bowl, mix the breadcrumbs, potato chips and paprika together. Dredge the cod fillets in the bread crumb mixture, covering both sides. Set these on a plate and refrigerate for at least an hour.

Prepare a 15½x10-inch pan by spraying with a non-stick vegetable spray. Cut the potatoes into thick lengthwise wedges. Place the canola oil and salt in a plastic bag and toss the potato wedges to coat. Arrange these on the prepared pan in a single layer. Bake in a pre-heated 400° oven for 35 to 40 minutes without turning. Potatoes should be tender and golden.

Reduce oven temperature to 350°. Place cod fillets in a baking pan lined with aluminum foil. Bake fish at 350° 4-6 minutes each side until golden and crispy. Serve with malt vinegar if desired. Serves 4.

## Nutrition Facts

Per serving: Calories 437 (25% calories from fat)  Fat 12 g (saturated fat 1.7 g)
Protein 31 g  Carbohydrates 51 g  Fiber 4 g  Cholesterol 62 mg  Sodium 913 mg.

*Fish & Shellfish*

# NORFOLK SHRIMP MEDITERRANEAN-STYLE

| | |
|---|---|
| 1 | tablespoon olive oil |
| 3 | cloves garlic, crushed |
| 1 | pound large shrimp, peeled and cleaned |
| 2 | tablespoons fresh lemon juice |
| 1 | teaspoon dried oregano |
| 2 | ounces feta cheese, crumbled |

Heat olive oil in a heavy skillet. Add garlic and cook 1 minute. Add shrimp and cook 2 minutes; turn and cook 1 minute more. Add lemon juice and oregano and cook until shrimp are done. (They will curl and turn bright pink). Do not overcook. Remove skillet from the heat and toss in feta cheese. The cheese will melt and become creamy, with some small chunks remaining. Serve immediately. Yield: 4 servings.

NOTE: This dish goes well served over orzo or couscous.

## Nutrition Facts

Per serving: Calories 217 (34% calories from fat) Fat 8 g (saturated fat 2 g) Protein 31 g  Carbohydrates 3.4 g  Fiber .1 g  Cholesterol 220 mg  Sodium 397 mg.

*Try a new high-fiber grain. Now there are quick-cook varieties of couscous, bulgar, quinoa and barley. Discover how really delicious they can be.*

# OUTER BANKS BLACKENED REDFISH

| | |
|---|---|
| 1 | teaspoon paprika |
| ½ | teaspoon dried sage |
| ½ | teaspoon dried cumin |
| ½ | teaspoon garlic powder |
| ½ | teaspoon granulated sugar |
| ½ | teaspoon salt |
| ¼ | teaspoon cayenne pepper (adjust if necessary) |
| ¼ | teaspoon onion powder |
| 4 | redfish (or farm-raised catfish) fillets |
| | Non-stick cooking spray |
| 1 | teaspoon olive oil |
| | Lemon slices |

Combine paprika, sage, cumin, garlic powder, sugar, salt, cayenne pepper and onion powder in a 1-gallon food storage bag. Seal bag and shake vigorously until spices are well-blended. Shake 1 fillet at a time until lightly coated with mixture. Coat a large non-stick skillet with cooking spray. Heat over medium-low and add olive oil, heating until hot. Sauté fillets 4-5 minutes until lightly blackened on one side. Carefully turn with spatula and cook 4-5 minutes longer, or until fish feels firm and is opaque at the thickest part. Serve with lemon slices. Yield: 4 servings.

## Nutrition Facts

Per serving:  Calories 307 (28% calories from fat)  Fat 9 g (saturated fat 1.3 g) Protein 48 g Carbohydrates 5.7 g Fiber 1 g Cholesterol 107 mg Sodium 1358 mg.

*Don't worry about substituting margarine for butter. Both are equal in "bad" fats and should be avoided as much as possible. Instead, use olive or canola oil for cooking and a diet tub to spread.*

# RHODE ISLAND CLAM CAKES

| | |
|---|---|
| 1 | cup seasoned seafood breader |
| 1 | cup flour |
| 4 | teaspoons baking powder |
| 1 | teaspoon salt |
| ½ | teaspoon pepper |
| | Egg substitute equivalent to 2 eggs |
| 1 | cup 1% milk |
| ½ | pint clams, in their liquor |

In a medium bowl, blend together the seafood breader, flour, baking powder, salt and pepper. Add in the milk and clams with their liquor. Toss gently to mix all. Using your hands, shape meatball-size rounds and place on a baking pan that is lined with aluminum foil. Press down to flatten to ½-inch thickness. Spray clam cakes with vegetable cooking spray and place in a preheated 350° oven for 25 to 30 minutes, or until done. Clam cakes should be crisp and golden on the outside. Yield: 4 clam cakes.

NOTE: This recipe is easy to double for heartier appetites.

## Nutrition Facts

Per serving: Calories 327 (8% calories from fat) Fat 2.7 g (saturated fat .7 g) Protein 15.5 g Carbohydrates 60 g Fiber 3.5 g Cholesterol 13 mg Sodium 1227 mg.

# SALMON STEAKS WITH LEMON-MUSTARD SAUCE

| | |
|---|---|
| 3 | tablespoons dry white wine |
| 2 | tablespoons fresh lemon juice |
| 2 | tablespoons reduced-fat mayonnaise |
| 2 | teaspoons Dijon mustard |
| 1 | teaspoon paprika |
| ¼ | teaspoon garlic powder |
| 1 | teaspoon black pepper |
| 4 | (6-ounce) salmon steaks |
| | Fresh lemon wedges |

In a small bowl, whisk together wine, lemon juice, mayonnaise, mustard, paprika and garlic powder; cover and chill until ready to cook.

Brush fish with marinade and sprinkle pepper over both sides of each salmon steak. Coat a food rack with cooking spray and place on a pre-heated grill over high heat (400 - 500°). Place salmon steaks on rack and cook with grill cover down 3 to 4 minutes on each side, or until fish flakes easily with a fork. Spoon remaining sauce over each fillet and serve with lemon wedges. Yield: 4 servings.

## Nutrition Facts

Per serving:  Calories 275 (42% calories from fat)  Fat 12.5 g (saturated fat 2 g) Protein 34 g  Carbohydrates 3 g  Fiber .3 g  Cholesterol 95 mg  Sodium 176 mg.

# SANTA CRUZ SHRIMP OR CRAB ENCHILADAS

| | |
|---|---|
| 1 | cup mild (or hot) salsa |
| ⅓ | cup light sour cream |
| 1 | cup 1% cottage cheese |
| 2 | tablespoons 1% milk |
| 1 | garlic clove, minced |
| ¼ | teaspoon salt |
| ⅓ | cup chopped green onion |
| 8 | (7-inch) flour tortillas |
| 4 | ounces low-fat Monterey Jack cheese, shredded |
| ¾ | pound fresh medium shrimp, shelled and cleaned or substitute crab meat |
| 2 | tablespoons fat-free Parmesan cheese |

In a small mixing bowl, combine salsa and sour cream; set aside. Combine cottage cheese, milk, garlic and salt in a food processor and blend till mixture is smooth; set aside. Spread 1 tablespoon of salsa mixture over each tortilla. Top each with shredded cheese, seafood and all but 1 tablespoon green onion.

Prepare a 12" x 7½" x 2" baking dish by spraying with non-stick cooking spray. Heat oven to 350°. Spoon remaining salsa mixture into prepared pan. Roll tortillas and place seam-side down, in prepared baking dish. Pour cottage cheese mixture over tortillas and sprinkle with Parmesan cheese. Bake, uncovered, in pre-heated oven for 25 to 30 minutes or till heated through. Sprinkle with remaining 1 tablespoon of green onion and serve. Yield: 8 tortillas.

## Nutrition Facts

Per serving: Calories 246 (28% calories from fat)  Fat 7.5 g (saturated fat 3.7 g)
Protein 18 g  Carbohydrates 25 g  Fiber .1 g  Cholesterol 65 mg  Sodium 880 mg.

## SEA SCALLOP BROCHETTES WITH ROASTED PEPPERS

1 ½   pounds large sea scallops
4   tablespoons olive oil, divided
1   tablespoon fresh lemon zest
½   teaspoon black pepper
4   large assorted red and yellow bell peppers
1   tablespoon red wine vinegar
1   tablespoon fresh lemon juice
1   tablespoon chopped fresh parsley
¼   teaspoon dried oregano
  Salt to taste

Prepare wooden skewers by soaking them in water at least 30 minutes and set aside. In a large bowl, combine scallops, 1 tablespoon of olive oil, lemon zest and black pepper and set aside to season. Pre-heat the broiler.

Cut each pepper in half lengthwise, removing stems, seeds and ribs. Place cut side down on a baking sheet. Broil until blackened on the top edge. This should take about 6-10 minutes. Remove and transfer the peppers to a paper bag, close tightly and let them cool for about 10 minutes. Remove and peel off the skin (which will come off quite easily), and cut long pepper strips about ¾-inch wide. Wrap a pepper strip around the outer edge of each scallop to completely encircle and thread 3 pepper-wrapped scallops onto a skewer, securing the peppers with the skewer as you thread. Place the filled skewers on a foil-lined broiling pan.

In a small bowl, whisk together the remaining olive oil, vinegar, lemon juice, parsley and oregano. Season to taste with salt and additional pepper if desired. Place skewers under the broiler about 6 inches from the heat. Broil approximately 3 minutes a side, or until scallops are done. Transfer them to a serving dish and drizzle them with the dressing. Serve immediately. Yield: 6 servings or 12 appetizer servings.

### Nutrition Facts

Per serving: Calories 211 (43% calories from fat)  Fat 10 g (saturated fat 1.3 g)
Protein 20 g  Carbohydrates 10 g  Fiber 2.4 g  Cholesterol 37 mg  Sodium 185 mg.

*Fish & Shellfish*

# SHRIMP IN LEMON GINGER CREAM SAUCE

1 ½   pounds fresh large or jumbo shrimp
½     cup non-fat half & half or non-dairy creamer
⅓     cup low-fat chicken broth
2     teaspoons cornstarch
½     teaspoon grated gingerroot
½     teaspoon grated lemon peel
3     teaspoons salted butter, divided
      Salt and pepper to taste
¼     cup dry white wine
¼     cup sliced green onion

Peel and devein shrimp, leaving tails on and set aside.

In a small saucepan, heat the creamer and chicken broth over medium heat. Add the cornstarch, ginger and lemon peel and stir to thicken. Drop 2 teaspoons butter into saucepan and set mixture aside as butter melts.

Heat a non-stick skillet over medium heat. Spray skillet with vegetable cooking spray and return to heat. Melt the remaining teaspoon butter and sauté shrimp until they are almost cooked. (Shrimp will turn translucent pink). Season to taste with salt and pepper. Add ¼ cup white wine and steam shrimp until they finish cooking. (Shrimp will curl when fully cooked). Remove shrimp to serving dish or individual plates. Give the lemon ginger cream sauce a final stir to incorporate the melted butter and pour over the cooked shrimp. Top with green onion and serve immediately. Yield: 4 servings.

NOTE: This is a very elegant dish, especially when served over couscous with a green vegetable.

## Nutrition Facts

Per serving: Calories 258 (30% calories from fat) Fat 7 g (saturated fat 2 g) Protein 22 g  Carbohydrates 14 g  Fiber .3 g  Cholesterol 209 mg  Sodium 276 mg.

## SURFSIDE STEAMER POT SEAFOOD FEAST

|       | Water and beer for steaming |
|-------|-----------------------------|
| ½ | cup Old Bay Seasoning |
| 3 | pounds mixed seafood (crabs, shrimp, clams and mussels) |
| 4 | ears fresh corn in the husk |
| 8 | medium-size red potatoes |
| ½ | cup chopped fresh parsley |

In a large steamer pot with a raised rack at least 2 inches high, add equal amounts of water and beer to just below the level of the steamer rack. Layer potatoes, crabs and corn, sprinkling the crabs with seafood seasoning. Cover and steam for 20 minutes. Add additional layers of shrimp, clams and mussels, sprinkling each layer with seasoning. Continue to steam seafood another 15 minutes until the crabs are red, shrimp turn pink and clams and mussels open. Discard any that do not. Garnish with parsley and serve with your favorite seafood sauce. Makes 4 servings.

### Nutrition Facts

Per serving:  Calories 542 (12% calories from fat)  Fat 7.4 g (saturated fat 1 g)
Protein 69 g  Carbohydrates 48 g  Fiber 4 g  Cholesterol 302 mg  Sodium 792 mg.

## TUNA GRILLED WITH LEMON-CAPER SAUCE

| ½ | teaspoon salt |
|-------|-----------------------------|
| ½ | teaspoon freshly ground pepper |
| 2 | tablespoons olive oil |
| ¼ | cup fresh lemon juice |
| ½ | cup chopped fresh parsley |
| 4 | tablespoons capers, crushed |
| 2 | pounds tuna steaks |
|   | Fresh lemon wedges |

Whisk together in a small bowl salt, pepper, olive oil, lemon juice, parsley and crushed capers. Brush tuna steaks with mixture and allow to sit for at least 30 minutes.

Prepare a grill and cook tuna steaks over medium-high heat for 5 minutes, searing one side. Turn, brush with marinade and cook 3-4 minutes more or until fish is done. Remove and serve immediately with lemon slices. Yield: 6 servings.

### Nutrition Facts

Per serving: Calories 207 (27% calories from fat)  Fat 6 g (saturated fat 1 g)  Protein
35 g  Carbohydrates 1 g  Fiber .3 g  Cholesterol 68 mg  Sodium 227 mg.

# Desserts

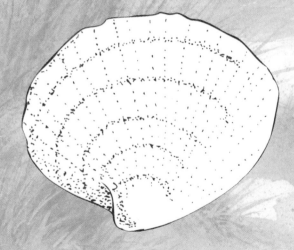

# Desserts

# AMARETTO & STRAWBERRY- TOPPED WHITE CAKE

| | |
|---|---|
| 4 | cups sliced fresh strawberries |
| 2 | tablespoons sugar |
| 1 | tablespoon amaretto liqueur |
| 1 | cup plus 2 tablespoons unbleached flour |
| ½ | cup sugar |
| 1 | teaspoon baking powder |
| ½ | teaspoon baking soda |
| ½ | cup plus 2 tablespoons nonfat buttermilk |
| 1 | egg white |
| 1 | teaspoon vanilla extract |

In a medium bowl, combine the strawberries, sugar and liqueur. Cover and chill for several hours.

In a large mixing bowl, combine the flour, sugar, baking powder and baking soda; stir to mix well. Stir in the buttermilk, egg white and vanilla. Spray a 9-inch round cake pan with nonstick cooking spray. Spread the batter evenly in the pan and bake at 325° for 15 to 20 minutes, or just until the center springs back when lightly touched. Cool the cake to room temperature, cut into wedges and serve each piece topped with the strawberry mixture. Yield: 8 servings.

## Nutrition Facts

Per serving: Calories 163 (2% calories from fat) Fat .5 g (saturated fat .1 g) Protein 3 g Carbohydrates 35 g Fiber 2 g Cholesterol 6 mg Sodium 135 mg.

*Dessertss*

# BAR HARBOR LEMON BISCOTTI

| | |
|---|---|
| 3 | cups unbleached flour |
| ½ | cup cornmeal |
| 2 | teaspoons baking powder |
| 3 | egg whites, lightly beaten |
| ½ | cup honey |
| 2 | tablespoons canola oil |
| 1 | teaspoon vanilla extract |
| ½ | cup lemon juice |

In a medium bowl, blend together flour, cornmeal and baking powder. In a large bowl, stir together egg whites, honey, oil and extract. Using a wire whisk, gradually stir the flour mixture into the egg white mixture and add enough lemon juice to make a pliable dough. Divide the dough in half and form each into a 12-inch roll.

Prepare a cookie sheet with parchment paper. Place the rolls apart from each other on the cookie sheet. Slightly flatten each roll to ½-inch in height. Bake in a pre-heated 350° oven 35 to 40 minutes or until tops are firm to the touch. Remove from the oven and allow to cool a few minutes. Using a serrated knife, cut slices ½-inch thick and place slices back on the cookie sheet, cut side down. Bake the biscotti for 10 to 15 minutes more, until they are light brown. Cool on a cooling rack. Yield: 40 biscotti.

## Nutrition Facts

Per serving: Calories 64 (12% calories from fat) Fat .8 g (saturated fat 0) Protein 1.5 g Carbohydrates 12.6 g Fiber .2 g Cholesterol 0 Sodium 30 mg.

*Yearning for a sweet cookie? Biscotti at 60 calories and 1 gram of fat fills the bill without leaving you feeling guilty.*

# BISCAYNE BAY HONEY OAT BROWNIES

¾   cup quick-cooking oats
¼   cup unbleached flour
¼   cup plus 2 tablespoons cocoa powder
½   cup sugar
⅛   teaspoon baking powder
⅛   teaspoon salt
6   tablespoons honey
¼   cup water
1   teaspoon vanilla extract
¼   cup chopped walnuts

Using one large mixing bowl, combine oats, flour, cocoa, sugar, baking powder and salt; stir to blend all ingredients. Add in the honey, water and vanilla extract, then stir to blend once more. Fold in the chopped walnuts.

Spray an 8-inch square baking pan with nonstick cooking spray. Spread the batter evenly in the pan, then bake in a pre-heated 325° oven for about 20 minutes, or until the edges are firm and the center is almost set. Remove from oven and cool to room temperature. Cut into 16 squares. Yield: 16 servings.

## Nutrition Facts

Per serving: Calories 86 (16% calories from fat)  Fat 1.7 g (saturated fat .3 g) Protein 1.5 g  Carbohydrates 18 g  Fiber 1 g  Cholesterol 0  Sodium 23 mg.

*If you crave an ice cream sundae, but not the fat and calories, simply substitute 1 cup of ice milk for the ice cream and 2 tablespoons frozen non-dairy whipped topping for whipped cream. You save 150 calories and 16 grams of fat.*

# CAPTIVA'S CHOCOLATE MOUSSE

| | |
|---|---|
| 1 | envelope unflavored gelatin |
| 2 | tablespoons unsweetened cocoa |
| 2 | eggs, separated |
| 2 | cups skimmed evaporated milk, divided |
| ¼ | cup sugar |
| 2 | packets artificial sweetener |
| 1½ | teaspoons vanilla |

In a medium-size saucepan, mix gelatin and cocoa. In a separate bowl, beat egg yolks with 1 cup milk. Blend into gelatin mixture. Let stand 1 minute to soften gelatin. Stir over low heat until gelatin is completely dissolved, about 5 minutes. Add remaining milk, sugar, sweetener and vanilla. Pour into a large bowl and chill, stirring occasionally, until mixture mounds slightly when dropped from a spoon.

In a separate large bowl, beat egg whites until soft peaks form; gradually add gelatin mixture and beat until mixture doubles in volume. This should take about 5 minutes. Chill mixture until it is slightly thickened. Turn into dessert dishes or a 1-quart bowl and chill until set. Yield: 8 servings.

## Nutrition Facts

Per serving:  Calories 102 (13% calories from fat)  Fat 1.5 g (saturated fat .5 g)
Protein 6.7 g  Carbohydrates 15 g  Fiber 0  Cholesterol 53 mg  Sodium 97 mg.

# CHARLESTON'S CHOCOLATE CHIP COOKIES

| | |
|---|---|
| 1 | packet Butter Buds (butter substitute) |
| ¼ | cup canola oil |
| 1 | cup sugar |
| 2 | eggs |
| 1 | teaspoon vanilla |
| 1 | cup all-purpose flour |
| 1 | cup whole-wheat flour |
| 1 | teaspoon baking soda |
| ½ | teaspoon salt |
| 1 | (6-ounce) package chocolate chips |
| 2 | cups 40% bran flake cereal |

Following the package directions, turn the Butter Buds into liquid. In a large mixing bowl, combine liquid Butter Buds, oil and sugar. Beat in the eggs and vanilla and stir until creamy. In a separate bowl, sift together the flours, baking soda and salt. Mix the dry ingredients into the egg mixture. Stir in the chocolate chips and cereal, blending all ingredients. Drop by rounded teaspoons onto a non-stick cookie sheet. Bake 8 to 10 minutes in a pre-heated 425° oven. Remove cookies from oven and immediately place on a wire rack to cool. Yield: 48 cookies.

## Nutrition Facts

Per serving: Calories 72 (29% calories from fat) Fat 2.4 g (saturated fat .7 g) Protein 1 g Carbohydrates 12 g Fiber .6 g Cholesterol 9 mg Sodium 73 mg.

# FRESH PEACH FROZEN YOGURT

| | |
|---|---|
| 1 | envelope unflavored gelatin |
| ¼ | cup cold water |
| 2 | cups fresh or frozen sliced peaches |
| ½ | cup sugar |
| 4 | cups plain yogurt |

In a small saucepan, sprinkle gelatin over cold water. Stir over low heat to dissolve. Place sliced peaches, sugar and yogurt in a blender container. Cover and process on high until smooth. Add dissolved gelatin; cover and blend again.

Pour mixture into a 13" x 9" glass baking dish. Freeze one hour, until mixture is partially frozen. Spoon into a large chilled bowl. With an electric mixer, beat on low speed about 30 seconds until mixture is smooth and airy, but not completely thawed. (Do not overbeat). Mixture should contain some ice crystals. Place in a 1½-quart freezer container. Cover and freeze 1 to 2 hours until mixture reaches the semi-frozen stage. Yield: about 1½ quarts.

## Nutrition Facts

Per serving:  Calories 98 (12% calories from fat)  Fat 1.3 g (saturated fat .8 g)
Protein 5 g  Carbohydrates 17 g  Fiber .5 g  Cholesterol 5 mg  Sodium 58 mg.

# GINGER SNAPS FROM HOLDEN BEACH

1 ⅓  cup whole wheat flour
¼    cup white granulated sugar
¾    teaspoon baking soda
½    teaspoon ginger
¼    cup molasses
3     tablespoons orange juice

Using one mixing bowl, combine the flour, sugar, baking soda and ginger, blending to mix well. Stir in the molasses and orange juice concentrate. Refrigerate dough for 30 minutes.

Coat a baking sheet with nonstick cooking spray. Roll the dough into 1-inch balls and place 1½ inches apart on the baking sheet. Using the bottom of a glass dipped in sugar, flatten the cookies to ¼-inch thickness.

Bake at 300° for about 12 minutes, or until lightly browned. Cool the cookies on the pan for 1 minute, then transfer them to a cooling rack for 10-15 minutes more. Yield: 24 cookies.

## Nutrition Facts

Per serving: Calories 43 (3% calories from fat) Fat .1 g (saturated fat 0) Protein 1 g  Carbohydrates 10 g  Fiber 1 g  Cholesterol 0  Sodium 41 mg.

# HUNTINGTON BEACH MAPLE SPICE CAKE

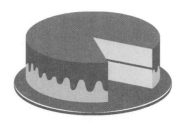

| | |
|---|---|
| 1 ⅓ | cups unbleached flour |
| 1 ⅓ | cups whole wheat flour |
| 1 | cup granulated sugar |
| 1 | tablespoon baking powder |
| 1 | teaspoon ground cinnamon |
| ½ | teaspoon ground ginger |
| ¼ | teaspoon nutmeg |
| 1 ⅓ | cups skim milk |
| ⅔ | cup maple syrup |
| 4 | egg whites (or equivalent) |
| | Confectioner's sugar for top |

Combine in a large mixing bowl the unbleached and whole wheat flour, sugar, baking powder, cinnamon, ginger and nutmeg. In a smaller bowl, mix milk, maple syrup and egg whites until blended. Stir the milk mixture into the dry ingredients, stirring with a wooden spoon to blend all together.

Prepare a 9x13-inch baking pan by spraying with nonstick cooking spray. Pour cake batter into pan and spread evenly into all corners. Bake in a pre-heated 350° oven for 30 to 35 minutes, or until a knife inserted into center of cake comes out clean. Cool to room temperature and sprinkle confectioner's sugar over top. Yield: 16 pieces.

## Nutrition Facts

Per serving: Calories 167 (2% calories from fat) Fat .4 g (saturated fat .1 g) Protein 4 g Carbohydrates 38 g Fiber 1.5 g Cholesterol 4 mg Sodium 69 mg.

# KIAWAH ORANGE PECAN TEA CAKE

| | |
|---|---|
| 2 | cups all-purpose flour |
| ¼ | cup sugar |
| 5 | packets artificial sweetener |
| 1 | tablespoon baking powder |
| ¼ | teaspoon salt |
| ⅓ | cup diet margarine |
| 1 | egg |
| ¾ | cup buttermilk |
| 1 | teaspoon vanilla |
| 1 | tablespoon grated orange rind |
| ¾ | cup finely chopped pecans |

In a medium-size bowl, sift together flour, sugar, sweetener, baking powder and salt, then sift a second time. Using a pastry blender or two knives, cut in the margarine until mixture resembles cornmeal. In a separate bowl, beat the egg until it becomes thick and lemon-colored. Add the buttermilk and vanilla; gradually add this to the dry ingredients. Stir in the orange rind and pecans. Pour batter into a 9-inch layer pan that has been sprayed with vegetable cooking spray. Bake in a pre-heated 375° oven for 25 to 30 minutes. Let stand 10 minutes, then turn out onto a cooling rack. Yield: 12 servings.

NOTE: This cake can be topped with a glaze of confectioner's sugar and a little orange juice for extra sweetness and flavor.

## Nutrition Facts

Per serving:  Calories 191 (44% calories from fat)  Fat 9.5 g (saturated fat 1.5 g)
Protein 4 g  Carbohydrates 22 g  Fiber 1.2 g  Cholesterol 18 mg  Sodium 182 mg.

*Dessertss*

# LAGUNA BEACH
# STRAWBERRY-BANANA CHARLOTTE

| | |
|---|---|
| 1 | (3-ounce) package ladyfingers |
| 2 | firm bananas, sliced |
| 24 | ounces fat-free cream cheese |
| 16 | envelopes sugar substitute |
| 1 | cup fat-free sour cream |
| 1 | teaspoon vanilla extract |
| ⅓ | cup water |
| 2 | envelopes unflavored gelatin |
| 1½ | cups pureed strawberries |
| 4 | envelopes sugar substitute |
| | Lite whipped topping for garnish (optional) |
| | Fresh strawberries for garnish |

Spray an 8x3-inch springform pan with vegetable cooking spray. Line the sides of the pan with the ladyfingers and the bottom of the pan with banana slices. In a large mixing bowl, beat the cream cheese with the sugar substitute, sour cream and vanilla until smooth. Soften gelatin in water, then heat over low until dissolved. Stir 2 tablespoons gelatin mixture into strawberry puree and blend in 4 envelopes sugar substitute. Blend remaining gelatin into cheese mixture. Pour 1 cup strawberry mixture over bananas, then pour in the cheese mixture. Add remaining strawberry mixture and swirl with a knife to get a marbled affect. Cover and chill until firm. Garnish with fresh strawberry slices and lite whipped topping if desired. Serves 12.

## Nutrition Facts

Per serving: Calories 139 (10% calories from fat) Fat 1.5 g (saturated fat .7 g) Protein 11 g Carbohydrates 21 g Fiber 2 g Cholesterol 12 mg Sodium 348 mg.

# LA JOLLA LEMON CHIFFON PIE

| | |
|---|---|
| 1 | envelope unflavored gelatin |
| 3 | tablespoons sugar |
| 1 | tablespoon grated lemon peel |
| 3 | packets artificial sweetener |
| ⅛ | teaspoon salt |
| 4 | eggs, separated |
| ½ | cup water |
| ⅓ | cup fresh lemon juice |

In a small saucepan, combine gelatin, sugar, lemon peel, sweetener and salt. Lightly beat egg yolks with water and lemon juice. Gradually stir the egg mixture into the gelatin and cook over low heat, stirring constantly, until slightly thickened. This should take about 10 minutes. Pour heated mixture into a large bowl and bring to room temperature. Cover and chill until mixture mounds slightly when dropped from a spoon, about 1½ hours. Beat egg whites until stiff peaks form. Gently fold into lemon mixture. Pour into a prepared graham-cracker pie crust. (Recipe follows). Cover and chill 5 hours, or until firm. Garnish top with additional lemon peel, if desired and serve. Yield: 8 servings.

## Nutrition Facts

Per serving: Calories 116 (28% calories from fat) Fat 3.7 g (saturated .8 g) Protein 5 g Carbohydrates 16 g Fiber .2 g Cholesterol 106 mg Sodium 155 mg.

# GRAHAM CRACKER CRUST

| | |
|---|---|
| 1 | cup crushed graham crackers (about 12) |
| 2 | tablespoons butter, melted |
| 2 | tablespoons plain yogurt |
| ¼ | teaspoon cinnamon |
| 1 | tablespoon sugar |

Preheat oven to 350°. In a small bowl, combine graham crackers, butter, yogurt, cinnamon and sugar. Press into a 9-inch pie plate or spring-form pan. Bake 7 minutes and set aside to cool while preparing filling. Yield: 1 pie crust.

## Nutrition Facts

Per serving: Calories 53 (19% calories from fat) Fat 1 g (saturated fat 0) Protein 1 g Carbohydrates 10 g Fiber 0 Cholesterol 0 g Sodium 85 mg.

# LEMON BLUEBERRY COFFEE CAKE

1 ¾    cups all-purpose flour
¾      cup sugar
1 ¾    teaspoons baking powder
½      teaspoon salt
2      teaspoons grated lemon peel
1      cup skim milk
½      cup egg substitute
3      tablespoons margarine, melted
1      cup fresh or frozen and thawed blueberries, well drained

Prepare a 9-inch by 1½-inch high pan, by spraying it with cooking spray. In a medium bowl, using a wooden spoon mix flour, sugar, baking powder, salt and lemon peel. Stir in milk, egg product and margarine until blended. Gently fold in blueberries and pour batter into prepared baking pan. Bake 20-25 minutes or until golden brown. Cool 10 minutes and remove from pan. You may drizzle the top with a sugar glaze, if desired. Yield: 15 servings.

## Nutrition Facts

Per serving:  Calories 130 (19% calories from fat)  Fat 2.8 g (saturated fat 1 g)
Protein 3 g  Carbohydrates 23 g  Fiber .7 g  Cholesterol 3 mg  Sodium 154 mg.

# MIAMI'S KEY LIME CHEESECAKE

| | |
|---|---|
| 1 | 32-ounce carton vanilla low-fat yogurt |
| ¼ | cup sugar |
| 2 | tablespoons cornstarch |
| 2 | tablespoons key lime juice |
| 2 | eggs, lightly beaten |

To do ahead: Drain yogurt to make yogurt cheese. (See recipe in this book).
Preheat oven to 325°. Lightly brush an 8-inch pie pan or 7-inch springform pan with vegetable oil. Place yogurt cheese in a medium-size bowl. Add sugar, cornstarch and lime juice, mixing gently until well blended. Add eggs and stir in.
Pour cheese mixture into the prepared pan, smoothing top with a spatula. Bake until center is set—about 25-30 minutes for a pie pan, 55-60 minutes for a springform. Cool slightly on a wire rack and refrigerate until chilled. Yield: 8 servings.

## Nutrition Facts

Per serving:  Calories 127 (22% calories from fat)  Fat 3 g (saturated fat 1.6 g)
Protein 8 g  Carbohydrates 17 g  Fiber 0  Cholesterol 61 mg  Sodium 103 mg.

# MOCHA FUDGE CAKE FROM MT. DESERT ISLAND

| | |
|---|---|
| 2 | cups unbleached flour |
| 1 ¼ | cups sugar |
| ½ | cup cocoa powder |
| 1 | teaspoon baking powder |
| ½ | teaspoon baking soda |
| ¼ | teaspoon salt (optional) |
| ½ | cup prune butter |
| 2 | tablespoons canola oil |
| 1½ | cups coffee at room temperature |
| 2 | teaspoons vanilla extract |
| ½ | cup chopped walnuts |
| 3-4 | tablespoons confectioner's sugar (optional) |

Combine flour, sugar, cocoa, baking powder, baking soda and salt (optional) in a large bowl and stir to blend ingredients. In a separate bowl, combine the prune butter, oil, coffee and vanilla, stirring to mix well. Add the prune mixture to the flour mixture and stir once more. Fold in the walnuts.

Prepare a 9 x 13-inch baking pan by spraying with vegetable spray. Spread the batter evenly in the pan and bake at 350° for 30-35 minutes, or until the top springs back when tested. Be careful not to overbake. When cake is done, remove from the oven and cool to room temperature. Sift the confectioner's sugar over the cake, cut into squares and serve. Yield: 16 servings.

## Nutrition Facts

Per serving: Calories 175 (21% calories from fat) Fat 4 g (saturated fat .5 g) Protein 3 g Carbohydrates 33 g Fiber .8 g Cholesterol 0 Sodium 92 mg.

# NEW BERN BANANA SPICE CAKE

| | |
|---|---|
| 1 | packet Butter Buds |
| 1½ | cups whole-wheat flour |
| 1 | cup all-purpose flour |
| 1½ | cups sugar |
| 1 ¼ | teaspoons baking powder |
| 1 ¼ | teaspoons baking soda |
| 1½ | teaspoons cinnamon |
| ¾ | teaspoon nutmeg |
| ½ | teaspoon salt |
| ½ | teaspoon ground cloves |
| ⅔ | cup buttermilk |
| 1 ¼ | cup ripe bananas, mashed |
| 2 | eggs |

Following package directions, turn Butter Buds into liquid and set aside. Prepare a 9 x 13-inch baking pan by spraying with vegetable cooking spray. In a medium-sized bowl, sift together the flours, sugar, baking powder, baking soda and spices. In a large bowl, combine liquid Butter Buds, buttermilk, bananas and eggs. Using an electic mixer, beat on low speed about 1 minute. Add dry ingredients gradually, beating until all ingredients are well blended. Pour batter into prepared baking pan.

Bake in a pre-heated 350° oven, 35-40 minutes, or until done. Transfer pan to a cooling rack. When cake is cooled, slice into 18 pieces and remove to a serving dish. Yield: 15 servings.

NOTE: This cake goes well served with lite whipped topping.

## Nutrition Facts

Per serving: Calories162 (8% calories from fat) Fat 1.4 g (saturated fat .5 g) Protein 4 g Carbohydrates 35 g Fiber 2 g Cholesterol 30 mg Sodium 161 mg.

*Sorbets are more flavor intense than fruit-flavored ice creams and at 1/3 the calories, you certainly won't miss the fat.*

# POACHED BANANAS WITH VANILLA FROZEN YOGURT

| | |
|---|---|
| 4 | ripe bananas |
| ½ | cup orange juice |
| 1 | cup apple juice |
| 1 | tablespoon vanilla extract |
| 1 | cinnamon stick |
| ¼ | teaspoon nutmeg |
| 2 | cups frozen vanilla yogurt |

Peel bananas, slice lengthwise and set aside. Combine the orange juice, apple juice, vanilla and cinnamon stick in a saucepan and bring to a simmer on medium heat. Add the bananas and cook covered about 10 minutes, or until the bananas are tender. Place bananas equally onto 4 serving plates and ladle sauce over each. Sprinkle with nutmeg and place a scoop of frozen vanilla yogurt on each one. Divide cinnamon stick in 4 equal pieces and use as a garnish. Serve immediately. Yield: 4 servings.

## Nutrition Facts

Per serving: Calories 251 (3% calories from fat) Fat .8 g (saturated fat .3 g) Protein 6 g  Carbohydrates 56 g  Fiber 3 g  Cholesterol 2 mg  Sodium 66 mg.

# RUMSON RASPBERRY CREPES

|       |                                                     |
|-------|-----------------------------------------------------|
| ¼     | cup skim milk                                       |
| 2     | tablespoons water                                   |
|       | Egg substitute equal to 2 eggs                      |
| ¼     | cup flour                                            |
| 3     | cups fresh raspberries, or 2 (10-ounce) packages frozen |
| 6     | packets sugar substitute                            |
| 2     | tablespoons raspberry or orange liqueur             |
|       | Confectioner's sugar for garnish                    |

In a small mixing bowl, blend milk and water together. Beat in eggs, then blend in flour gradually, whisking until smooth. Spray a crepe pan with vegetable cooking spray and heat over medium heat. Spread approximately 2 tablespoons into the hot crepe pan, spreading evenly and cooking until edges turn brown. Cook each crepe, spraying pan after each one is cooked, then turn out of pan and set aside until all batter is used.

Combine raspberries, sugar substitute and liqueur. Fill each crepe with raspberries, roll up jelly-roll style and place onto a serving dish. Top with remaining raspberry juice and sprinkle with confectioners sugar. Yield: 6 servings or 12 crepes.

## Nutrition Facts

Per serving: Calories 86 (9% calories from fat) Fat 1 g (saturated fat 0) Protein 3.6 g Carbohydrates 17 g Fiber .2 g Cholesterol 0 mg Sodium 33 mg.

*Make up a mix of dried fruits and roasted soy bean nuts for a quick take-a-long snack in a bag.*

# SEAL COVE STRAWBERRY POPPY SEED MUFFINS

| | |
|---|---|
| ¾ | cup skim milk |
| ⅓ | cup applesauce |
| ¼ | cup egg substitute |
| 2 | cups all-purpose flour |
| ¾ | cup sugar |
| 1 | tablespoon poppy seeds |
| 2 | teaspoons baking powder |
| ½ | teaspoon salt |
| 1 | cup fresh strawberries cut up (frozen may be used) |

Prepare a muffin tin by spraying with cooking spray. Into a large bowl, place milk, applesauce and egg substitute product and beat gently to blend. Add in flour, sugar, poppy seeds, baking powder and salt, stirring just until dry ingredients are blended. Gently stir in strawberries. Place batter into 12 muffin cups so that each cup is almost full.

Bake in a pre-heated oven for 20 minutes or until muffins are done. Cool a few minutes before removing from pan. Yield: 12 muffins.

## Nutrition Facts

Per serving: Calories 145 (5% calories from fat) Fat .8 g (saturated fat .1 g) Protein 4 g Carbohydrates 31 g Fiber 1 g Cholesterol .3 mg Sodium 153 mg.

*To cut back on fat with home-baked goods, substitute applesauce or prune puree for up to half the amount of butter, margarine or oil called for in the recipe.*

# SPONGECAKE WITH STRAWBERRIES & CREAM

½   cup cornstarch
2   tablespoons all-purpose flour
1   teaspoon baking powder
3   eggs
⅓   cup sugar
4   packets artificial sweetener
12  medium fresh strawberries
2   cups lite whipped topping

In a medium bowl, sift together cornstarch, flour and baking powder. In a separate, larger bowl, beat eggs with electric mixer until foamy. Beat in sugar and sweetener gradually, continuing to beat until the mixture is very thick and lemon colored. Gently fold in dry ingredients, a few tablespoons at a time, gently mixing to thoroughly blend. Fold batter into two 8-inch round layer pans that have been sprayed with vegetable cooking spray. Place pans in a pre-heated 375° oven and reduce the heat to 350°. Bake 15 minutes, or until cake begins to shrink from the sides of pan and top springs back when lightly tested. Let stand 1 or 2 minutes. Loosen sides and turn onto cooling rack. When cake has cooled, spread whipped topping over each cake layer. Put one on top of the other and top with strawberries. Yield: 8 servings.

## Nutrition Facts

Per serving:  Calories 141 (18% calories from fat)  Fat 2 g (saturated fat .6 g)
Protein 3 g  Carbohydrates 26 g  Fiber 1 g  Cholesterol 79 mg  Sodium 63 mg.

# VANILLA CUSTARD FROM PLEASANT BAY BEACH

| | |
|---|---|
| 2 | eggs |
| 2 | packets artificial sweetener |
| 1 | teaspoon vanilla |
| 1 ½ | cups skim milk, scalded |
| | Pinch of nutmeg |

In a medium-size bowl, beat the eggs, slightly. Add sweetener and vanilla, then slowly stir in the milk. Pour mixture into 4 custard cups and set into a shallow pan filled with 1 inch of hot water. Sprinkle with nutmeg and place in a pre-heated 350° oven for 30 minutes or until knife inserted into center comes out clean. Yield. 4 (½-cup) servings.

## Nutrition Facts

Per serving: Calories 79 (31% calories from fat) Fat 3 g (saturated fat 1 g) Protein 7 g Carbohydrates 5.5 g Fiber 0 Cholesterol 108 mg Sodium 85 mg.

# VENICE BEACH VANILLA SUGAR COOKIES

| | |
|---|---|
| 1 | yellow moist supreme cake mix |
| ¼ | cup egg white product |
| ¼ | cup water |
| ¼ | cup unsweetened applesauce |

Pour cake mix into a large mixing bowl, breaking up any lumps with a fork. In a smaller mixing bowl, combine egg white, water and applesauce, stirring to blend all ingredients. Add the egg white mixture to the cake mix, stirring with a wooden spoon until batter is well blended. Drop rounded teaspoons of cookie dough onto a cookie sheet that has been sprayed with non-stick cooking spray. Bake in a pre-heated 350° oven for 6 minutes. Remove cookie tray and using a spatula, press down on each cookie to flatten. Bake another 6 to 8 minutes, until cookies are done. They will be light brown on top and firm to the touch. Yield: 4 dozen cookies.

NOTE: Try this recipe with other cake mixes to invent some interesting types of cookies.

## Nutrition Facts

Per serving: Calories 46 (20% calories from fat) Fat 1 g (saturated fat .4 g) Protein .6 g  Carbohydrates 8.7 g  Fiber .3 g  Cholesterol 0  Sodium 70 mg.

# WHALE COVE JAM & OATMEAL JUMBLES

|  |  |
|---|---|
| ¾ | cup whole wheat flour |
| ¾ | cup unbleached flour |
| 2 | cups quick-cooking oats |
| ¾ | cup light brown sugar |
| 1 ¼ | teaspoons baking soda |
| ½ | teaspoon ground cinnamon |
| ¾ | cup jam or fruit preserves (any flavor) |
| ½ | cup egg beaters |
| ¼ | cup water |
| 1 | teaspoon vanilla extract |
| ¾ | cup dark raisins, chopped fruit or nuts |

Using one large bowl, combine the flours, oats, brown sugar, baking soda and cinnamon. Stir to mix all ingredients. Add the jam or preserves, egg beaters, water and vanilla; stir once more to mix all ingredients. Stir in the fruit or nuts.

Coat a baking sheet with nonstick cooking spray. Drop rounded teaspoon-fuls of dough onto the baking sheet, placing them 1½-inches apart. Slightly flatten each cookie with the tip of a spoon.

Bake in a pre-heated 275° oven for about 18 minutes, or until lightly browned. Let cookies sit on the pan for 1 minute, then transfer them to wire cooling racks to cool. Yield: 60 jumbles.

## Nutrition Facts

Per serving: Calories 46 (4% calories from fat) Fat .2 g (saturated fat 0)
Protein .9 g Carbohydrates 10 g Fiber .7 g Cholesterol 0 Sodium 29 mg.

# Tips for
# Healthy Eating

1.  Build a core diet consisting of nutrient-dense foods such as fruits, vegetables, whole grains, low-fat dairy products, lean meat, poultry and seafood.

2.  Smart eating starts with smart selections at the grocery store. Substitute low-fat or fat-free foods for the ones you already use. Your favorite recipes will be leaner and you will never know the difference.

3.  A balanced diet keeps blood sugar on an even keel. This means less temptation to over-eat at mealtimes and more energy to improve mental and physical functions.

4.  The best way to analyze your current eating habits is to keep a food diary of everything you eat for at least two days. Since most people miscalculate their nutritional intake, you may discover that your diet is not what you think it is.

5.  Compare your daily food intake to the US Department of Agriculture's Food Guide Pyramid to see how you "measure up".

6.  How many calories do you really need? Divide your weight in pounds by 2.2 and multiply that number by 21.6. Then multiply that number by 1.3 if sedentary, 1.5 if lightly active or 1.9 if very active. The resulting number is a close estimate of the total number of calories you need to maintain your current weight.

7.  You can adjust your weight by adding or subtracting 500 calories to or from your diet each day. Adding calories will result in a one-pound gain, while subtracting calories will result in a one pound loss per week.

8.  Good nutrition doesn't mean giving up your favorite foods. It is more a matter of portion size to consider in diet context. A good motto is: "more of the best, less of the rest".

9.  Large restaurant portions distort our perception of what is a normal serving size. It is always a good practice to eat half and bring the other half home.

10. To envision normal portions, imagine the palm of your hand as a 3-ounce portion of protein and a closed fist as 1 cup of rice or veggies. Envisioning these portion sizes will keep us in line.

11. When eating out, choose wisely. Order salad with the dressing on the side, meat, poultry and seafood that is grilled or broiled and not fried,

baked potatoes with vegetable toppings, steamed vegetable side dishes and fruit for dessert.

12. For good diet habits, nutritionists suggest dividing your dinner plate into three sections. Fill half of your plate with vegetables and fruits, one-quarter with grains or whole grains and the remaining quarter with protein food.

13. Not eating enough lowers your body metabolism and you may store most of the calories you take in as fat.

14. Pay attention to your appetite. Eat only when you're hungry, not just because food is there.

15. Eat slowly, so your brain has time to send messages to your body that you're no longer hungry.

16. Be wary of "low-fat" food claims. Knowing what a serving is can help determine whether the food really is low in fat. (To qualify, a food must contain no more that 30% fat calories, or 10% saturated fat).

17. Saturated fat increases blood cholesterol in most individuals. Too high a serum cholesterol level increases your chance of heart disease.

18. Since the fat you eat is the fat you wear, just eat low-fat for a healthy lifestyle.

19. Why is water good for you? It has no calories or fat, fills you up when you drink it with meals and allows the body to carry out all of it's functions. So drink up—8 glasses a day.

20. Flavored seltzer—a great stand-in for soft drinks and soda saves the calories and counts towards the recommended consumption of 8 glasses of water per day.

21. Leading a sedentary life will jeopardize your health. For this reason get active. A brisk walk three times a week is a good way to start a moderate aerobic program.

22. Walking—the body's best all-around shaper—just 20 minutes skims off 80-120 calories from your daily intake. The faster you go—the more you burn.

23. To maintain a happy body weight, maintain a lean muscle-to-fat ratio. Light weight-training exercises done in as little as 1 hour per week will keep metabolism humming.

24. Lost muscle mass and hormonal shifts in mid-life can affect calorie burning ability by as much as 50 calories per day. But 10 minutes of extra daily activity can ward off a potential 5-pound yearly weight gain.

25. Weight-bearing activities slow down bone loss that leads to osteoporosis and will cause the body to build strong bones that will resist fractures in later years.

26. Moderate weight-training has been touted as the "fountain of youth" because it reverses many signs of aging and allows physical fitness to be maintained.

27. Think of ways to add physical activity to your daily life. For example, park your car further away from your destination and walk the extra distance.

28. Don't allow your scale to gather dust. People who maintain a healthy body weight, weigh themselves frequently and take immediate action at the first sign of weight gain.

29. Ninety per-cent of all people who maintain a healthy body weight exercise regularly.

30. Managing a lifetime plan for healthy eating and maintaining an active life-style seem to be the keys to health and longevity. If you have not already begun, you can start your plan now—what have you got to lose?

# Index

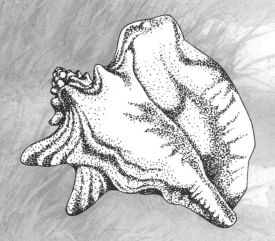

## Appetizers & Beverages

## Breads & Breakfast

## Soups & Salads

## Vegetables & Casseroles

# Notes

# Notes

To order additional copies, make checks payable to:
Father & Son Publishing, Inc. and mail to:
4909 North Monroe Street • Tallahassee, Florida 32303

Please send me _____ copies of *Lean Beach Cuisine* @ 12.95 plus $3.00 each for postage and handling. Florida residents add 7% sales tax.
Enclosed is my check or money order for $ _____

Name _____

Address _____

City_____ State _____ Zip _____

MasterCard/Visa Card # _____

Exp. date _____ Signature _____

— — — — — — — — — — — — — — — — — — — — — — — — — — — —

To order additional copies, make checks payable to:
Father & Son Publishing, Inc. and mail to:
4909 North Monroe Street • Tallahassee, Florida 32303

Please send me _____ copies of *Lean Beach Cuisine* @ 12.95 plus $3.00 each for postage and handling. Florida residents add 7% sales tax.
Enclosed is my check or money order for $ _____

Name _____

Address _____

City_____ State _____ Zip _____

MasterCard/Visa Card # _____

Exp. date _____ Signature _____

— — — — — — — — — — — — — — — — — — — — — — — — — — — —

To order additional copies, make checks payable to:
Father & Son Publishing, Inc. and mail to:
4909 North Monroe Street • Tallahassee, Florida 32303

Please send me _____ copies of *Lean Beach Cuisine* @ 12.95 plus $3.00 each for postage and handling. Florida residents add 7% sales tax.
Enclosed is my check or money order for $ _____

Name _____

Address _____

City_____ State _____ Zip _____

MasterCard/Visa Card # _____

Exp. date _____ Signature _____